Canadian

Fast-Fix
5 Ingredient Cooking

BY
Elizabeth Baird
and the Canadian Living® Test Kitchen

TELEMEDIA

Canada
am

Robert
ROSE

Produced for Canadian Living®

Canadian Living® Fast-Fix 5 Ingredient Cooking

Canadian Cataloguing in Publication Data

Canadian living fast fix 5 ingredient cooking

ISBN 1-896503-38-1 (book)
ISBN 1-896503-40-3 (videotape)
ISBN 1-896503-42-X (book & videotape)

I. Quick and easy cookery. I. Title:
Canadian living fast fix five ingredient cooking.

TX833.5.C36 1997   641.5'55   C96-932363-8

TEXT AND COVER DESIGN, EDITORIAL, PAGE COMPOSITION AND VIDEO CAPTURES	MATTHEWS COMMUNICATIONS DESIGN
PHOTOGRAPHER:	CHRISTOPHER DEW
FOOD STYLIST:	LUCIE RICHARD
PROPS STYLIST:	CHARLENE ERRICSON
INDEXER:	BARBARA SCHON

Props used in photography supplied by:
TABLE OF CONTENTS, TORONTO   *Dinnerware, linens, utensils & glassware*
SURROUNDINGS FLORAL DESIGN INC., TORONTO   *Plants & clay planters*
THE COMPLEAT KITCHEN, TORONTO   *Cookware, glassware & dishes*
FOLLY, TORONTO   *Dinnerware, glassware & accessories*

Distributed in Canada by:
Stoddart Publishing Co. Ltd.
34 Lesmill Road
North York, Ontario
M3B 2T6

ORDER LINES
Tel: (416) 445-3333
Fax: (416) 445-5967

Produced by: Robert Rose Inc., 156 Duncan Mill Road, Suite 12
Toronto, Ontario, Canada M3B 2N2   Tel: (416) 449-3535

Printed in Canada

234567 ML 99 98

Contents

"Make it easy."

This is what I hear from readers across Canada. And that is exactly what the 60 recipes in *Fast-Fix 5 Ingredient Cooking* do. They take the fuss out of preparing weeknight suppers — the most important time for uncomplicated, delicious and healthy family meals. And nothing takes the fuss out of cooking faster than cutting back on the number of ingredients. That means less taking out and putting away, less measuring and less chopping. All the dishes call for just five supermarket-available items, not counting the water, salt, pepper and oil, which everyone has on hand.

Best of all, the dishes — made with satisfying full-flavored ingredients — fit into healthy-eating guidelines. This makes it even easier for the home cook to choose a recipe without the worry of whether or not it's a nutritious choice. Twelve of the recipes are also on the companion video. There, I share techniques, tips and menu ideas, plus shopping and make-ahead suggestions to make cooking and sitting down to that all-important family supper easy and fun.

Elizabeth Baird
Food Director, Canadian Living

ACKNOWLEDGMENTS

Special thanks go to *Canadian Living*'s senior editors Beverley Renahan and Julia Armstrong; members of the test kitchen, with special mention for Emily Fernandes, test kitchen manager Donna Bartolini and Riki Dixon; associate food director Daphna Rabinovitch; organizer par excellence Olga Goncalves; editor-in-chief Bonnie Baker Cowan; publisher/vice-president Caren King.

Sincere appreciation is extended to photographer Christopher Dew; food stylist Lucie Richard; props stylist Charlene Erricson; Sharyn Joliat and Barbara Selley of Info Access (1988) Inc.; Robert Dees, president, Robert Rose Inc.; the ever-encouraging Sidney Cohen, executive producer, CTV, and his hard-working crew; Glen Dickout, marketing manager, CTV; Sharon and Peter Matthews, Matthews Communications Design.

— E.B.

Soups

Soups

Soup TIPS

- *Keep a store of broth or stock on your emergency shelf in the pantry. To make your own stock, save and freeze left-over poultry bones, then follow the recipe for Chicken Stock, page 10.*

- *When using canned broth, or powdered or cubed stock, do not salt the dish until it is cooked and you have had a chance to taste it.*

- *Save cooking liquid from mild-flavored vegetables such as carrots, green beans and potatoes. If you have any left-over vegetables, you can always add them at the last moment to an already-prepared soup.*

- *When reheating soups, especially ones with a base of pasta, beans, peas or lentils, you will need to add more liquid, water, milk or stock, depending on the soup.*

- *To add a smoky flavor to soup, add a little diced smoked ham, chicken, turkey or pastrami.*

- *Always taste a soup just before serving; flavorings such as herbs may need a boost.*

- *Dress up a bowl of soup with toppings. Easy garnishes include a dollop of thick yogurt, a sprinkle of crumbled feta or freshly grated Asiago or Parmesan cheese, chopped green onions or fresh herbs, sliced mushrooms, slivered toasted almonds, chopped tomatoes or sweet peppers, or anything that offers freshness or contrasting color and crunch.*

▼ CREAMY CLAM AND CORN CHOWDER
(RECIPE, PAGE 9)

MENU

Lentil Vegetable Soup

Whole Wheat Bagels

Tossed Greens with Ranch Dressing

TIP

If buying mixed vegetables in bulk or using a combo of your own, count on 2-⅓ cups (575 mL).

•

Rinse off frozen vegetables in a sieve before adding to soup in order to get rid of any ice or excess water.

MAKES 6 SERVINGS

PER SERVING

calories	225
protein	11 g
fat	5 g
carbohydrate	36 g
source of fibre	very high
source of iron	excellent

Lentil Vegetable Soup

This hearty soup, made with green or brown lentils, is one to enjoy for supper. Or for lunch, pack it in a vacuum bottle or reheat it in the microwave. A sprinkle of cheese over the top wouldn't be amiss.

2	Onions, chopped	2
4 tsp	Chili powder	20 mL
1 cup	Green or brown lentils	250 mL
1	Can (19 oz/540 mL) stewed tomatoes	1
1	Bag (300 g) frozen regular diced mixed vegetables	1

1. In Dutch oven or large heavy saucepan, heat 2 tbsp (25 mL) vegetable oil over medium heat; cook onions and chili powder, stirring occasionally, for about 5 minutes or until softened.

2. Add lentils, stirring until well coated. Add 3 cups (750 mL) water; bring to boil. Reduce heat to low; cover and simmer, stirring occasionally, for about 20 minutes or until lentils are almost tender.

3. Stir in tomatoes, breaking up chunky pieces with spoon. Bring to boil over medium-high heat; reduce heat to medium and cook, covered, for about 15 minutes or until lentils are completely tender.

4. Add vegetables and return to simmer; cook for 5 minutes. Season with ½ tsp (2 mL) each salt and pepper.

step by step

In heavy-bottomed saucepan, cook green onions, stirring often, for 3 minutes.

Add drained baby clams...

... and creamed corn; cook for 3 minutes, stirring occasionally.

Stir in milk. Season with a little freshly ground pepper.

Add herbed cream cheese, a little at a time, stirring gently after each addition until blended.

Ladle soup into heated bowls. Sprinkle with reserved green onion.

Creamy Clam and Corn Chowder

Clams are a regular storehouse of flavor and a traditional partner with corn in a clam bake. Here, for the ultimate in convenience, they unite in a soothing soup.

4	Green onions	4
2	Cans (each 5 oz/142 g) baby clams	2
1	Can (10 oz/284 mL) creamed corn	1
1-3/4 cups	1% milk	425 mL
1/2 cup	Light herbed cream cheese (4 oz/125 g)	125 mL

1. Trim green onions and slice thinly; reserve 1/4 cup (50 mL) of the green part for garnish.

2. In large heavy saucepan, heat 1 tbsp (15 mL) vegetable oil over medium heat; cook onions for 3 minutes, stirring often.

3. Drain clams and add to pan along with corn; cook for 3 minutes, stirring occasionally.

4. Stir in milk and 1/4 tsp (1 mL) pepper. Add cheese by spoonfuls, stirring gently after each addition until blended. Cook, stirring often, until steaming. Serve sprinkled with reserved green onion.

MAKES 4 SERVINGS

PER SERVING	
calories	255
protein	15 g
fat	13 g
carbohydrate	23 g
source of calcium	good
source of iron	excellent

MENU

Tortellini and Green Pea Soup

Crusty Italian Bread

Sliced Tomato, Green Pepper and Cucumber Salad

TIP

Instead of peas, you can use your own diced fresh vegetables or a mix of frozen bulk or packaged ones. Or shred 4 cups (1 L) washed fresh spinach or Swiss chard leaves and stir into the soup just long enough to wilt before serving.

VARIATION

Vegetarian Tortellini and Green Pea Soup: For a vegetarian version, replace chicken stock with vegetable stock. Omit ham. Add ½ cup (125 mL) diced sweet red pepper.

MAKES 4 SERVINGS

PER SERVING

calories	360
protein	28 g
fat	10 g
carbohydrate	36 g
source of fibre	high
source of calcium	good
source of iron	good

Tortellini and Green Pea Soup

Here's a soup that "eats" like a pasta dish. It's worthwhile keeping a few packages of cheese tortellini in the freezer for supper when time is short.

5 cups	Chicken stock or broth	1.25 L
1	Pkg (8 oz/250 g) cheese tortellini	1
2 cups	Frozen peas	500 mL
1 cup	Diced smoked ham or kielbasa	250 mL
⅓ cup	Freshly grated Parmesan cheese	75 mL

1. In large saucepan, bring stock to boil over high heat.
2. Add tortellini, stirring to prevent sticking to bottom; return to boil. Reduce heat and simmer for about 5 minutes or until almost tender.
3. Add peas and ham; simmer for about 5 minutes or until steaming.
4. Sprinkle with Parmesan cheese to serve.

Chicken Stock

Chicken stock or broth from cans, powder or cubes can be very salty. To make your own is easy, takes virtually no effort or time and is well worth trying. Save and freeze the bones when deboning chicken breasts or buy chicken backs and necks. When you have about 8 cups (2 L), place in pot with enough cold water to cover 1-¼ times. Bring to boil; reduce heat and simmer, skimming off any scum. When scum ceases rising to the top, add 1 each chopped onion, carrot and outside celery stalk with leaves, 1 bay leaf and 1 sprig fresh thyme or ½ tsp (2 mL) dried thyme. Simmer gently, uncovered, for about 1-½ hours, stirring up from bottom from time to time. Strain through fine sieve, discarding bones and vegetables. Makes about 6 cups (1.5 L) stock.

MENU

Split Pea Soup with Lemon and Cumin

Carrot Sticks and Tzatziki Dip

Kaiser Rolls

TIP

Pack any leftovers in an airtight container. Then you have a choice of freezing the soup for later, taking it for lunch or serving it again with sandwiches.

Look for yellow split peas in a bulk-food store, or in the supermarket where dried legumes and beans are stocked.

Split Pea Soup with Lemon and Cumin

Dapple a bowl of this Mediterranean soup with croutons, chopped fresh parsley or green onions.

2	Onions, chopped	2
1 tbsp	Ground cumin	15 mL
2	Lemons	2
2 cups	Yellow split peas	500 mL
6 cups	Chicken or vegetable stock	1.5 L

1. In Dutch oven or large heavy saucepan, heat 1 tbsp (15 mL) extra-virgin olive oil over medium heat; cook onions and cumin, stirring occasionally, for 5 minutes or until softened and aromatic.

2. Meanwhile, with zester or coarse side of grater, remove outer rind from lemons.

3. In sieve, rinse and drain split peas; add to onion mixture along with lemon rind and stock. Bring to boil; reduce heat, cover and simmer, stirring occasionally, for about 30 minutes or until peas are softened.

4. Pour about one-quarter of the soup into blender or food processor; purée until smooth. Stir purée into soup to thicken.

5. Squeeze lemons; strain juice into soup. Season with $1/4$ tsp (1 mL) pepper. Heat through until steaming.

MAKES 6 SERVINGS

PER SERVING	
calories	315
protein	22 g
fat	5 g
carbohydrate	48 g
source of fibre	very high
source of iron	excellent

MENU

All-Dressed Pizza Soup

Breadsticks

Tossed Greens with Dijon Vinaigrette

TIP

Choose a pasta or spaghetti sauce with lots of flavor, such as one with sun-dried tomatoes, mushrooms or basil.

•

Instead of mozzarella cheese, try ¼ cup (50 mL) freshly grated Parmesan or Asiago cheese.

MAKES 4 SERVINGS

PER SERVING	
calories	310
protein	13 g
fat	14 g
carbohydrate	36 g
source of fibre	high
source of calcium	good
source of iron	good

All-Dressed Pizza Soup

Here are all the familiar flavors of a favorite classic pizza in a bowl.

1	Onion, chopped	1
1	Sweet yellow or green pepper, diced	1
3 cups	Sliced mushrooms (about 8 oz/250 g)	750 mL
1	Jar (700 mL) meatless pasta sauce	1
1 cup	Shredded part-skim mozzarella cheese	250 mL

1. In Dutch oven or large heavy saucepan, heat 1 tbsp (15 mL) extra-virgin olive oil over medium heat; cook onion, stirring occasionally, for 2 minutes or until softened slightly.

2. Add yellow pepper and mushrooms; cook, stirring often, for about 5 minutes or until most of the liquid is evaporated.

3. Stir in pasta sauce and 2-½ cups (625 mL) water; bring to boil. Reduce heat and simmer for about 15 minutes or until vegetables are tender. Season with pinch of pepper.

4. Sprinkle with mozzarella cheese to serve.

Chicken

Chicken

▼ HONEY CITRUS–GLAZED CHICKEN
(RECIPE, PAGE 17)

Chicken TIPS

- *Chicken can be stored in the refrigerator for up to 48 hours, ground chicken for up to 24 hours, or in the freezer up to six months.*

- *Unpack chicken from grocery bags as soon as possible. Place packages on a tray in the coldest part of the refrigerator.*

- *Either cook chicken the same day it is bought or wrap and store it on a clean plate. This ensures that any juices from the chicken do not drip onto other foods, especially those eaten raw.*

- *Do not refreeze thawed, uncooked chicken.*

- *Once cooked, chicken can be refrigerated immediately without waiting for it to cool, or it can be safely frozen.*

- *You can keep cooked chicken in the refrigerator for up to two days, handy for quick meals.*

- *After working with raw or partially cooked chicken, clean all utensils and cutting board thoroughly with hot soapy water and rinse well. Then make up enough of a solution of one part chlorine bleach to four parts water to cover board and utensils; let stand for at least 45 seconds before rinsing thoroughly.*

MENU

Chicken Mu Shu

Romaine Salad with Sliced Orange and Radishes

TIP

Supermarket or deli-available ready-cooked chicken will make quick work of this supper. Just reduce the hoisin sauce by half and eliminate the marinating time.

Chicken Mu Shu

Nicely glazed and flavored with hoisin, tender chicken makes an outstanding filling for easy roll-ups.

4	Chicken breasts	4
½ cup	Hoisin sauce	125 mL
4	Green onions, chopped	4
1 tbsp	Grated gingerroot	15 mL
6	8-inch (20 cm) flour tortillas	6

1. With gentle tugging motion, pull skin from chicken breasts. Place, bone side down, in shallow glass dish.

2. In small bowl, stir together half each of the hoisin sauce and green onions; stir in ginger, 1 tbsp (15 mL) vegetable oil and ¼ tsp (1 mL) pepper.

3. Spread hoisin mixture evenly over chicken, rubbing into flesh. Turn chicken over; cover and refrigerate for at least 4 hours or for up to 24 hours, turning occasionally to coat.

4. Arrange chicken, bone side down, in shallow roasting pan. Roast in 375°F (190°C) oven for about 40 minutes or until edges are crisped and chicken is no longer pink inside. Let cool slightly; remove meat from bone and cut lengthwise into strips.

5. Meanwhile, wrap tortillas in foil; heat in 350°F (180°C) oven for 10 minutes. Unwrap and spread with remaining hoisin sauce. Divide chicken and remaining green onions among tortillas; roll up.

MAKES 6 SERVINGS

PER SERVING	
calories	295
protein	23 g
fat	7 g
carbohydrate	34 g
source of iron	good

step by step

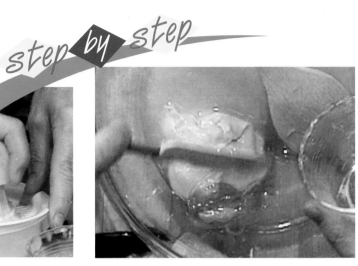

With zester, remove outer rind from orange and lemon; squeeze and strain juice.

In glass bowl, combine rind and juice with mustard, honey and pepper.

With gentle tugging motion, remove skin from chicken. Add chicken to marinade, turning to coat thoroughly.

Place marinated chicken breasts on foil-lined baking sheet, meaty side down. Spoon some marinade on top. Bake for 20 minutes.

Turn chicken and brush with remaining marinade, then continue baking until golden brown.

Arrange chicken on serving platter and serve with pan juices.

MENU

Honey Citrus–Glazed Chicken

Rice with Corn and Red Pepper Confetti

Broccoli Salad

TIP

Instead of chicken breasts, you can use 4 whole chicken legs or 8 chicken thighs, adding a few minutes to cooking time. The dark meat of chicken legs and thighs will always be slightly pink, even when fully cooked. Legs and thighs are done when juices run clear when chicken is pierced.

•

When the rind of citrus fruit is being used in a dish, scrub the fruit with a soft vegetable brush and detergent; rinse well.

MAKES 4 SERVINGS

PER SERVING	
calories	230
protein	29 g
fat	2 g
carbohydrate	23 g

Honey Citrus–Glazed Chicken

Roasting chicken breasts with a generous dollop of mustard, honey and citrus just adds to the pleasure of this versatile food.

1	Seedless orange	1
Half	Lemon	Half
¼ cup	Dijon mustard	50 mL
¼ cup	Liquid honey	50 mL
4	Chicken breasts	4

1. With zester or grater, remove outer rind from orange and lemon; squeeze and strain juice. In large glass dish, combine orange and lemon rind and juice, mustard, honey and ¼ tsp (1 mL) pepper. Set aside.

2. With gentle tugging motion, pull skin from chicken; discard. Add chicken to dish, turning to coat all over. Cover and refrigerate for at least 4 hours or for up to 24 hours, turning occasionally.

3. Reserving marinade, arrange chicken, meaty side down, on foil-lined rimmed baking sheet. Spoon some of the marinade over top. Bake in 375°F (190°C) oven for 20 minutes.

4. Turn chicken and brush with remaining marinade; bake, basting with pan juices 3 or 4 times, for 10 to 20 minutes longer or until golden brown and juices run clear when chicken is pierced. Serve with pan juices.

MENU

Thai Curry Stir-Fry

Long-Grain or Basmati Rice

Steamed Sugar Snap or Snow Peas

TIP

Red curry paste, seemingly exotic a few years ago, has followed the expansion and popularity of Thai restaurants across Canada and can be bought in pouches or cans in Asian and specialty grocery stores in many parts of the country. An ultimate convenience ingredient, this long-keeping curry paste contains hot peppers, galingal and lemongrass — all essential for authentic flavors.

•

For speed and convenience, you can buy chicken breasts already boned and skinned.

MAKES 4 SERVINGS

PER SERVING	
calories	185
protein	28 g
fat	6 g
carbohydrate	3 g

Thai Curry Stir-Fry

Flavor is what counts in a stir-fry, and this one gets a robust boost of it from the aromatic ingredients in Thai curry paste. It's lightly cooked before stir-frying with the chicken to round out and balance its taste.

4	Chicken breasts	4
2 tsp	Red curry paste	10 mL
8	Green onions, chopped	8
2 tsp	Thai fish sauce	10 mL
1/2 tsp	Granulated sugar	2 mL

1. With gentle tugging motion, pull skin from chicken breasts. With sharp knife and starting at long straight side, insert knife close to bone. With short strokes and keeping knife as close to bone as possible, cut away flesh. Cut meat across the grain into very thin strips. Set aside.

2. In wok or large skillet, heat 1-1/2 tsp (7 mL) vegetable oil over high heat. Add red curry paste; stir for about 30 seconds or until broken up and darkened slightly.

3. Immediately add chicken; stir-fry to separate and coat with curry. Stir-fry until firm and no longer pink inside, about 5 minutes. Transfer to plate.

4. Add 1-1/2 tsp (7 mL) vegetable oil to wok; stir-fry green onions and fish sauce for about 1 minute or until softened.

5. Return chicken to wok along with sugar; stir-fry just to mix and heat through.

MENU

Roasted Chicken Breasts with Sage and Prosciutto

Soft Polenta with Chopped Green Onion

Sliced Tomato Salad

TIP

Instead of sage, you can take your pick of herbs to season this chicken; thyme, basil and marjoram are delicious choices.

In warm weather, cook these breasts on the barbecue. Instead of using crumbled dried sage, place whole fresh sage leaves on the chicken before wrapping it in prosciutto.

Roasted Chicken Breasts with Sage and Prosciutto

This fast and easy five-ingredient meal will leave you savoring the memories long after the dishes are done and guests have gone home.

2 tbsp	Dijon mustard	25 mL
Dash	Hot pepper sauce	Dash
4	Boneless skinless chicken breasts	4
1 tsp	Crumbled dried sage	5 mL
8	Thin slices prosciutto ham (5 oz/150 g)	8

1. Combine mustard and hot pepper sauce; brush all over chicken. Sprinkle with sage and $1/4$ tsp (1 mL) pepper.

2. Wrap chicken with prosciutto, covering as much as possible. Place on foil–lined rimmed baking sheet; brush top with 1 tsp (5 mL) vegetable oil.

3. Bake in 375°F (190°C) oven for about 20 minutes or until prosciutto is crisped and juices run clear when chicken is pierced.

MAKES 4 SERVINGS

PER SERVING	
calories	195
protein	34 g
fat	5 g
carbohydrate	1 g

Cooking Chicken

Chicken should be cooked until no longer pink inside and juices run clear when chicken is pierced. Here is a guide for 2 boneless skinless chicken breasts, about 4 oz (125 g) each.

- Bake in 375°F (190°C) oven for 20 minutes.
- Grill over medium-high heat, covered and turning once, 10 to 12 minutes.
- Pan-fry in lightly greased skillet over medium heat for 15 minutes.
- Poach in water or chicken stock for 15 minutes.
- Microwave at High for 6 minutes.

MENU

Chicken and Zucchini Stir-Fry

Focaccia Bread

Honeydew Wedges

VARIATION

Chicken and Zucchini Pasta:
Before cooking the stir-fry, cook 2 cups (500 mL) penne in large pot of boiling salted water. Drain, reserving 1 cup (250 mL) of the cooking liquid. Cook the stir-fry and add to pasta. Add reserved liquid to skillet and bring to boil, stirring to scrape up brown bits. Cook until slightly reduced; pour over pasta mixture and toss to coat. Makes 2 servings.

MAKES 2 SERVINGS

PER SERVING

calories	240
protein	29 g
fat	9 g
carbohydrate	12 g

Chicken and Zucchini Stir-Fry

A generous grating of Parmesan or other flavorful cheese or a sprinkle of red wine vinegar or balsamic vinegar is delicious over the top of this colorful and quick skillet supper. For extra substance, do as we have done for the cover photo and toss the sauce with penne pasta (see variation, this page).

1	Onion	1
2	Small zucchini (or 1 large)	2
Half	Sweet red pepper	Half
2	Boneless skinless chicken breasts	2
2 tbsp	Chopped fresh basil (or 1 tsp/5 mL dried)	25 mL

1. Cut onion in half from stem to root end; place cut side down and cut lengthwise into thin strips. Trim zucchini; cut in half lengthwise, then crosswise into thin slices. Cut red pepper into thin strips. Cut chicken across the grain into thin strips.

2. In large nonstick skillet, heat 1-1/2 tsp (7 mL) vegetable oil over medium heat; cook onion, stirring often, for about 8 minutes or until golden.

3. Add zucchini, red pepper, half of the basil and 1/4 tsp (1 mL) each salt and pepper. Cook, tossing often, for about 4 minutes or until slightly softened. Transfer to plate.

4. Add 1-1/2 tsp (7 mL) vegetable oil to pan. Increase heat to medium-high; cook chicken, stirring often, for about 5 minutes or until browned and no longer pink inside.

5. Return vegetables to pan; toss to combine and heat through. Sprinkle with remaining basil to serve.

Fish

Fish

▼ ROASTED VEGETABLES WITH FISH
(RECIPE, PAGE 25)

Fish TIPS

- *Fish is one of the fastest and easiest ingredients for week-night and weekend meals.*

- *Choose fish that's firm, glistening and has a fresh, not fishy, fragrance. Don't be afraid to substitute one fish for another if it looks fresher.*

- *Buy fish from a fish store or supermarket with a high turnover and ask the fishmonger when supplies come in so that you can plan your seafood menus accordingly.*

- *Frozen fish is often the best choice for weekday meals. Blocks of fillets or individually frozen ones are handy to keep in the freezer. With the help of the microwave oven, defrosting and cooking fish takes very little time. Or transfer frozen fish to a plate or platter and defrost overnight or during the day in the refrigerator.*

- *No matter whether you're roasting, pan-frying, grilling, poaching or steaming fish, it takes only about 10 minutes at high heat per 1 inch (2.5 cm) of thickness.*

- *To test for doneness, insert a fork into the thickest part of the fish and twist gently. If the fish is opaque, moist and flakes easily, it is done. Avoid overcooking because fish continues to cook after it's removed from heat.*

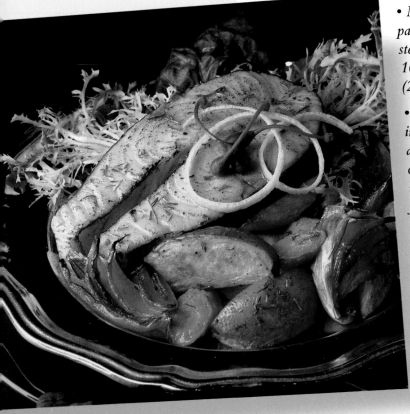

MENU

Shrimp with Tomato Sauce

Fluffy Rice

Just-Wilted Spinach or Swiss Chard

TIP

In growing season, replace the dried mint with fresh, choosing spearmint for the best flavor. You will need about 3 tbsp (50 mL) in all. Garnish the finished dish with sprigs of fresh mint.

Shrimp with Tomato Sauce

You may think mint is a surprising herb to combine with tomatoes and shrimp, but it's a delightful accent when you try them simmered together in a tasty sauce.

1	Large onion, chopped	1
1	Sweet yellow pepper, chopped	1
1 tbsp	Dried mint	15 mL
1	Can (28 oz/796 mL) tomatoes	1
1 lb	Cooked peeled small shrimp	500 g

1. In large skillet, heat 2 tbsp (25 mL) extra-virgin olive oil over medium heat. Add onion, yellow pepper and mint; cook, stirring often, for about 5 minutes or until vegetables are softened.

2. Add tomatoes, breaking up with spoon; simmer for 10 to 15 minutes or until thickened and reduced by about one-quarter.

3. Add shrimp; cook for 2 minutes or until heated through. Season with 1/4 tsp (1 mL) pepper.

MAKES 4 SERVINGS

PER SERVING

calories	290
protein	34 g
fat	10 g
carbohydrate	15 g
source of iron	excellent

step by step

Cut each potato into 6 uniform wedges: start by cutting potato in half, then cut each half into 3 equal wedges.

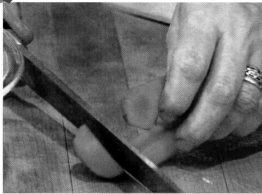

Peel and cut carrots into 1-inch (2.5 cm) lengths. To ensure uniform size, cut thicker pieces in half lengthwise.

Quarter onions lengthwise. Pat vegetables dry and place in bowl. Toss with oil, herbs, salt and pepper to coat evenly. Add salmon; toss gently to coat fish.

Transfer vegetables to foil-lined baking sheet and arrange in single layer. Roast until almost fork-tender.

Place salmon among cooked vegetables; roast until fish flakes easily and vegetables are tender and slightly crusted.

Transfer salmon to serving platter and surround with vegetables. Garnish with lemon wedges and fresh basil leaves.

Roasted Vegetables with Fish

Roasting is a great amplifier of flavors, making even simple vegetables such as carrots and onions sweet and succulent, and appropriate mates for filleted fish. Serve with lemon wedges.

4	**Red-skinned potatoes**	4
2	**Large carrots**	2
2	**Large onions**	2
1 tsp	**Dried basil or herbes de Provence**	5 mL
4	**Salmon steaks (6 oz/175 g each)**	4

1. Cut each potato into 6 wedges. Peel and cut carrots into 1-inch (2.5 cm) lengths. Cut onions into quarters from stem to root. Pat vegetables dry.

2. Place vegetables in large bowl. Sprinkle with 2 tbsp (25 mL) extra-virgin olive oil, basil and ½ tsp (2 mL) each salt and pepper; toss to coat evenly. Add salmon; toss again gently to coat fish.

3. Transfer salmon to plate and refrigerate. Arrange vegetables in single layer on large foil-lined rimmed baking sheet. Roast in 400°F (200°C) oven, turning once or twice, for 30 to 35 minutes or until almost fork-tender.

4. Nestle salmon among vegetables. Roast for about 15 minutes or until fish flakes easily when tested with fork and vegetables are tender and slightly crusted.

Oven-Fried Fish

Easy, easy, easy — that's the only way to describe these golden-crusted fillets.

½ cup	**Fine dry bread crumbs**	125 mL
1 tsp	**Dried basil**	5 mL
1 lb	**Fish fillets, about ½ inch (1 cm) thick**	500 g
3 tbsp	**Butter, melted**	50 mL
1	**Lemon**	1

1. In shallow dish, stir together bread crumbs, basil and ¼ tsp (1 mL) each salt and pepper.

2. Brush fillets with butter. Dip into bread crumb mixture to coat both sides, pressing in crumbs firmly.

3. Place fish in single layer on lightly greased rimmed baking sheet; drizzle with any remaining butter. Bake in top third of 500°F (260°C) oven for about 10 minutes or until golden and crusty and fish flakes easily when tested with fork.

4. Meanwhile, quarter lemon lengthwise; serve with fish to squeeze over top.

MAKES 4 SERVINGS

PER SERVING	
calories	240
protein	23 g
fat	11 g
carbohydrate	11 g

Oven Fries

Count on 1 medium white or sweet potato per person. Cut each in half lengthwise, then each half into 3 long wedges. In bowl, toss wedges with just enough vegetable oil to coat and salt and pepper to taste. Arrange in single layer on foil-lined rimmed baking sheet. Roast in 400°F (200°C) oven, turning once or twice, for about 40 minutes or until crisp on outside and tender inside.

Chili-Crusted Salmon Steaks

Roasting salmon or other fish with a spicy coating keeps the fish moist and adds a friskiness you may not get in a sauce or accompanying vegetable.

4	Salmon steaks (6 oz/175 g each)	4
1 tbsp	Chili powder	15 mL
1 tsp	Ground cumin or dried oregano	5 mL
2	Green onions, thinly sliced	2
½ cup	Diced sweet red or yellow pepper	125 mL

1. Place salmon on foil-lined rimmed baking sheet.

2. In small microwaveable bowl or saucepan, stir together chili powder, 1 tbsp (15 mL) vegetable oil, cumin and ¼ tsp (1 mL) salt. Cover and microwave at High for 45 seconds or heat until bubbling.

3. Brush chili mixture over both sides of salmon, coating evenly. Let stand for 30 minutes.

4. Roast in 500°F (260°C) oven, spooning pan juices over top, for 10 to 12 minutes or until fish flakes easily when tested with fork.

5. Serve sprinkled with green onions and red pepper.

MENU

Pan-Fried Fillets with
Chunky Tomato Salsa

Boiled New Potatoes

Steamed Green Beans

TIP

For a salsa that doesn't bite back, replace the jalapeño pepper with ⅓ cup (75 mL) diced sweet pepper such as Cubanelle, Shepherd or banana, or with diced green onion.

•

Coriander is also known as cilantro (from its Spanish origin) and Chinese parsley, names that trace this aromatic herb's many locations of cultivation and culinary exploration.

Pan-Fried Fillets with Chunky Tomato Salsa

Sauce, or "salsa" in Italian and Spanish, doesn't need to be complicated to complement good ingredients such as fresh fish. Try this salsa of chopped tomato, hot pepper and herbs over salmon, snapper, cod, swordfish, halibut, sea bass or pickerel, or even a simple pan-fried chicken breast.

2	Tomatoes	2
1	Jalapeño pepper, finely chopped	1
⅓ cup	Finely chopped fresh coriander or basil	75 mL
1 tbsp	Balsamic vinegar	15 mL
4	Fish fillets (1-½ lb/750 g total)	4

1. Core and dice tomatoes. In bowl, gently toss together tomatoes, jalapeño pepper, all but 3 tbsp (50 mL) of the coriander and vinegar; let salsa stand for up to 30 minutes.

2. Sprinkle fillets with ¼ tsp (1 mL) salt and remaining coriander.

3. In skillet large enough to hold fillets in single layer, heat 2 tsp (10 mL) extra-virgin olive oil; cook fillets, turning once, for about 6 minutes or until golden brown and fish flakes easily when tested with fork.

4. Top fillets with salsa to serve.

MAKES 4 SERVINGS

PER SERVING	
calories	255
protein	31 g
fat	12 g
carbohydrate	3 g

Pasta Sauces

Pasta Sauces

▼ ZUCCHINI TOSS
(RECIPE, PAGE 33)

Pasta TIPS

- *Count on 12 oz to 1 lb (375 to 500 g) pasta to serve four people.*

- *Water takes longer to come to the boil than most of these sauces take to make. Start heating the water in a covered pot as soon as you start meal preparation.*

- *Be sure to cook the pasta in a large pot with plenty of water — 10 to 12 cups (2.5 to 3 L) for each 8 oz (250 g) of pasta — increasing the water and size of pot according to the amount of pasta. Salt the water generously. You do not need to add oil to the water to prevent pasta from sticking together; stirring and cooking in plenty of water does this.*

- *Add pasta to boiling water, stirring to prevent it from sticking to the bottom of the pot. Cover just until it returns to boil. Time the pasta cooking from the moment the water boils.*

- *Pasta is ready to drain when it is tender but not mushy, and is slightly resistant to the bite, as the Italian term al dente suggests.*

- *Drain pasta in a colander, reserving some cooking liquid. Do not rinse the pasta because this prevents the sauce from sticking to it. Dump the pasta back into the cooking pot and add the sauce, stirring or tossing gently to coat evenly.*

- *If a moister dish is desired, add a little of the reserved cooking liquid.*

MENU

Red Pepper Pasta Sauce
with Radiatore

Steamed Green Beans
with Lemon

TIP

You will need 1 lb (500 g)
pasta for this sauce.

•

Reserve the liquid drained
from the roasted peppers and
use it to moisten the pasta after
tossing it with sauce, if desired.

•

If you have your own roasted
peppers, you will need about
1 cup (250 mL).

Red Pepper Pasta Sauce

A pasta shape such as radiatore or rotini is best because it will hold every last bit of this robust sauce. Sprinkle each serving with a little freshly grated hard cheese such as Parmesan, pecorino or Asiago.

4	**Cloves garlic, minced**	4
1	**Small onion, finely chopped**	1
1	**Jar (313 mL) roasted red peppers**	1
1	**Can (19 oz/540 mL) tomatoes**	1
2 tsp	**Crumbled dried basil or mint**	10 mL

1. In large skillet, heat 2 tbsp (25 mL) extra-virgin olive oil over medium heat; cook garlic and onion, stirring occasionally, for about 3 minutes or until softened.

2. Drain roasted peppers. In food processor or blender, purée peppers and tomatoes until almost smooth.

3. Add pepper mixture to skillet along with basil; bring to boil. Reduce heat and simmer, stirring often, for about 10 minutes or until thick enough to mound on spoon. Season with ¼ tsp (1 mL) each salt and pepper.

MAKES 3 CUPS (750 mL), ENOUGH FOR 4 SERVINGS

PER SERVING	
calories	120
protein	2 g
fat	7 g
carbohydrate	13 g

Roasted Peppers

Jars of roasted peppers are handy, but they are expensive. When there is an abundance of sweet red peppers (Shepherd are preferred for flavor), roast them in a 375°F (190°C) oven, turning often, for about 35 minutes or until skin loosens from flesh. Or grill or broil them for 20 to 30 minutes, turning as each side blisters and browns. Place in bowl; cover and let stand for about 10 minutes. Peel off skin; remove seeds and membranes.

step by step

In skillet, cook seasonings, then add sweet peppers and cook for 4 minutes.

Meanwhile, trim zucchini and, using grater over bowl, shred coarsely.

Add zucchini to skillet and sauté for 2 minutes or just until heated through.

Drain cooked pasta and transfer to serving bowl. Add zucchini mixture and cheese.

Toss together to coat pasta.

Serve immediately.

MENU

Zucchini Toss with Penne

*Tomato Wedges with
Black Olives*

TIP

You will need 4 cups (1 L) penne for this sauce.
Cook penne in lots of boiling salted water for about 8 minutes or until tender but still firm to the bite. Drain and place in large heated pasta bowl; add the zucchini sauce and cheese, then toss to coat the penne evenly.

•

You can also serve this as a cold pasta salad.

Zucchini Toss

Year-round, zucchini is inexpensive, and in the summer, there are countless ways to enjoy this colorful vegetable.

4	Cloves garlic, slivered	4
1 tsp	Dried Italian herb seasoning	5 mL
1	Each sweet red and orange pepper, chopped	1
3	Zucchini (1 lb/500 g total)	3
1/2 cup	Freshly grated pecorino, Asiago or feta cheese	125 mL

1. In skillet, heat 2 tbsp (25 mL) extra-virgin olive oil over medium heat; cook garlic, herb seasoning and 1/4 tsp (1 mL) coarsely ground pepper for 4 minutes, stirring occasionally.

2. Add red and orange peppers; cook for 4 minutes, stirring occasionally.

3. Meanwhile, trim and shred zucchini coarsely. Increase heat to medium–high; add zucchini to skillet and sauté for 2 minutes to heat through.

4. Toss zucchini mixture with pecorino cheese to serve.

**MAKES 4 CUPS (1 L),
ENOUGH FOR 4 SERVINGS**

PER SERVING	
calories	150
protein	4 g
fat	11 g
carbohydrate	10 g

MENU

Squash and Tomato Pasta Sauce with Rotini

Belgian Endive Salad with Orange Vinaigrette

TIP

You will need 1 lb (500 g) pasta for this sauce.

•

Unless you can see all or part of the words *Parmigiano Reggiano* stamped on the label of Parmesan cheese, it is not the real thing. Although a chunk of it may seem expensive, you amortize the cost over the number of weeks you have it in the fridge, handy for grating just what you need over pasta, an omelette, rice, baked potatoes, Caesar salad and soup.

MAKES 6-½ CUPS (1.625 L), ENOUGH FOR 4 SERVINGS

PER SERVING	
calories	245
protein	5 g
fat	8 g
carbohydrate	45 g
source of fibre	very high
source of iron	good

Squash and Tomato Pasta Sauce

Raisins and cinnamon add a certain Sicilian flair to this sauce, which pairs well with rotini or pasta shells. A sprinkling of freshly grated Parmesan cheese is an optional touch.

2	Onions, chopped	2
4 cups	Cubed peeled butternut squash (about 1-½ lb/750 g)	1 L
¼ tsp	Cinnamon	1 mL
1	Can (28 oz/796 mL) tomatoes	1
½ cup	Golden raisins	125 mL

1. In large skillet, heat 2 tbsp (25 mL) extra-virgin olive oil over medium heat; cook onions, stirring occasionally, for about 5 minutes or until softened.

2. Add squash and cinnamon, stirring to coat well.

3. Stir in ⅓ cup (75 mL) water; cover and cook for about 10 minutes or just until squash is almost tender and water is evaporated.

4. Stir in tomatoes, breaking up with spoon. Bring to boil; reduce heat and simmer, stirring occasionally, for about 15 minutes or until sauce is thickened and squash is tender.

5. Add raisins and ¼ tsp (1 mL) each salt and pepper.

MENU

Puttanesca Sauce with Pasta Shells

Boston Lettuce Salad with Creamy Cucumber Dressing

TIP

You will need 1 lb (500 g) short pasta for this sauce.

Buy oil-cured olives in jars or in bulk in Greek, Italian or Portuguese grocery stores. Although Kalamata olives are a delight in a salad or for nibbling, they are too vinegary for this sauce. Likewise, avoid bland canned black olives.

MAKES 3-½ CUPS (875 mL), ENOUGH FOR 4 SERVINGS

PER SERVING	
calories	305
protein	6 g
fat	18 g
carbohydrate	33 g
source of fibre	high

Puttanesca Sauce

This robust tomato-based sauce spiked with garlic, capers, anchovies and black olives is not for the timid. But it is for pasta lovers who want satisfaction. Serve over short pasta such as shells or fusilli to cup the chunky olives and capers. Sprinkle with Parmesan cheese, if desired.

4	Cloves garlic, slivered	4
5	Anchovies, chopped (or 2 tbsp/25 mL anchovy paste)	5
1	Jar (700 mL) tomato pasta sauce	1
¾ cup	Pitted oil-cured black olives	175 mL
¼ cup	Drained capers	50 mL

1. In large skillet, heat 1 tbsp (15 mL) extra-virgin olive oil over medium heat; cook garlic and anchovies, stirring and mashing with back of fork, for 4 minutes or until garlic is softened and anchovies are blended into oil.

2. Add pasta sauce; bring to boil, stirring often. Reduce heat and simmer for 5 minutes.

3. Add olives and capers; simmer for 5 minutes. Season with ¼ tsp (1 mL) pepper.

Tortellini with Broccoli and Cheese

Mixed Greens with Lemon Vinaigrette

TIP

You can use frozen tortellini as well as fresh; however, it will take about 2 minutes longer to cook. Vary the dish by using meat-filled tortellini instead of cheese-filled.

Tortellini with Broccoli and Cheese

Cheese-filled tortellini are almost a meal in themselves. Nevertheless, they go up a notch in taste with broccoli, carrots and cheese.

1	**Pkg (8 oz/250 g) fresh tortellini**	1
2	**Carrots, chopped**	2
3 cups	**Coarsely chopped (bite-size) broccoli or asparagus, or peas**	750 mL
1 cup	**Low-fat milk**	250 mL
½ cup	**Low-fat herbed cream cheese**	125 mL

1. In large pot of boiling salted water, cook tortellini and carrots for 5 minutes.

2. Add broccoli; cook for 2 minutes or until vegetables and tortellini are tender. Drain well and set aside, reserving ½ cup (125 mL) of the cooking liquid.

3. In same pot, heat milk with cream cheese over medium heat, stirring until cheese is melted.

4. Return tortellini mixture to pot; toss to coat well, adding a little of the reserved cooking liquid to moisten if necessary.

MAKES 4 SERVINGS

PER SERVING	
calories	295
protein	14 g
fat	11 g
carbohydrate	36 g
source of fibre	high
source of calcium	good

Meat

Meat

Meat TIPS

- *Calculate 4 oz (125 g) raw boneless meat per serving. This amount looks about as big as a pack of cards. When serving a steak, cut it crosswise into thin slices rather than serving it in chunks; slices make a more generous-looking serving, and provide people more flexibility about the amount they serve themselves.*

- *If meat has been frozen, defrost it in the refrigerator, never on the counter.*

- *When bringing home meat from shopping, unpack it immediately and place it on a tray or large plate. Store it in the coldest part of the refrigerator. Use ground beef, pork or lamb within a day of the package date and steaks or chops within three days.*

- *When slicing meat, cut it across the grain for the most tender results.*

- *After removing steaks or chops from heat, tent loosely with foil and let the meat stand for a few minutes to permit the juices to redistribute through the meat before serving.*

- *To slice meat thinly for dishes such as stir-fries or scaloppine, be sure that your knife is very sharp. It helps if the meat has been firmed up by freezing for 30 to 60 minutes.*

- *For well-browned meats, such as for stews, avoid overcrowding the pan and make sure that the surface of the meat is thoroughly dry before adding it to the pan. Paper towels make good blotters.*

- *To remove fat from the skillet, tip the skillet and drain or spoon off fat. Or use a baster.*

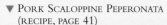

▼ PORK SCALOPPINE PEPERONATA
(RECIPE, PAGE 41)

MENU

Creamy Dill Hamburgers

Honey-Glazed Carrots

Warm Focaccia

TIP

For burgers, lean ground pork is an excellent alternative to beef.

•

Other herbs such as basil work well in this sauce, too, so try adding your favorite instead of the dill. To use dry herbs, reduce the amount to 1 tsp (5 mL), and freshen up the dish with some chopped fresh parsley.

MAKES 4 SERVINGS

PER SERVING

calories	235
protein	23 g
fat	13 g
carbohydrate	4 g
source of iron	good

Creamy Dill Hamburgers

Get those burgers out of the buns and serve them as a main course with this creamy mushroom sauce. Garnish the plate with watercress for a special effect.

1 lb	Lean ground beef	500 g
1 tbsp	Chopped fresh dill (or 1 tsp/5 mL dried dillweed)	15 mL
1 tbsp	Worcestershire sauce	15 mL
3 cups	Sliced mushrooms (8 oz/250 g)	750 mL
¼ cup	Light sour cream	50 mL

1. In bowl, mix together beef, 1 tsp (5 mL) of the dill, the Worcestershire sauce, ½ tsp (2 mL) pepper, ¼ tsp (1 mL) salt and ¼ cup (50 mL) cold water. Form into 4 patties about ¾ inch (2 cm) thick.

2. Heat nonstick skillet over medium–high heat; brush lightly with a little vegetable oil. Brown patties on both sides. Reduce heat to medium; cook for 10 to 15 minutes or until no longer pink inside. Transfer to plate.

3. Drain off any fat from pan. Add 2 tsp (10 mL) vegetable oil; increase heat to medium–high. Add mushrooms; cook, stirring often, until browned and juices are evaporated.

4. Reduce heat to medium. Pour in ¼ cup (50 mL) water. Stir in sour cream and remaining dill; cook, stirring, until blended and hot.

5. Return patties to skillet to warm through and coat with sauce.

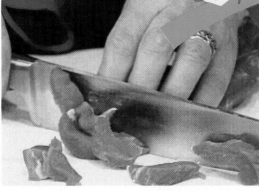

Trim off any fat from pork; cut into thin slices.

Toss pork in flour to coat, separating strips and shaking off excess flour.

Stir-fry peppers and half of the herb seasoning in a little oil over medium-high heat. Transfer to plate.

Cook pork, in batches, with remaining herb seasoning, just until browned. Add to peppers.

Add wine to deglaze skillet, stirring to scrape up brown bits from bottom. Bring to boil, stirring constantly, for about 2 minutes or until slightly thickened.

Return pork and peppers to skillet; cook, tossing until heated through and coated with sauce.

TIP

If you can't find colorful sweet peppers or they are too expensive, use three green peppers.

•

You can substitute dried basil or marjoram for the Italian herb seasoning.

Pork Scaloppine Peperonata

Plenty of colorful peppers combine with thin pork cutlets for a quick and stylish supper.

2	**Small pork tenderloins (about 1 lb/500 g total)**	2
1/3 cup	**All-purpose flour**	75 mL
1	**Each sweet red, yellow and green pepper**	1
1-1/2 tsp	**Dried Italian herb seasoning**	7 mL
3/4 cup	**Dry white wine or chicken stock**	175 mL

1. Trim off any fat from pork; cut into 1/4-inch (5 mm) thick slices. Cut into finger-size strips. Pour flour into bag. Add pork, in batches, and toss to coat, separating strips and shaking off excess flour. Set aside in single layer on waxed paper.

2. Core, seed and remove membranes from red, yellow and green peppers; cut into finger-size strips.

3. In large skillet, heat 2 tsp (10 mL) vegetable oil over medium-high heat; stir-fry peppers with half of the herb seasoning for about 8 minutes or until starting to soften. With slotted spoon, transfer to platter.

4. Add just enough oil to skillet to coat bottom. Cook pork and remaining herb seasoning, in batches if necessary, until browned on both sides. Add to peppers.

5. Pour wine and 1/2 cup (125 mL) water into skillet, stirring to scrape up brown bits from bottom of pan. Boil, stirring constantly, for about 2 minutes or until slightly thickened.

6. Return peppers and pork to pan; cook, stirring, just until heated through and coated with sauce. Season with 1/4 tsp (1 mL) each salt and pepper.

MAKES 4 SERVINGS

PER SERVING	
calories	235
protein	27 g
fat	6 g
carbohydrate	13 g
source of iron	good

MENU

*Knackwurst and Cabbage
One-Pot Supper*

Rye Bread

Carrot Salad

TIP

Besides knackwurst, any smoked sausage takes nicely to this dish.

•

You can add 2 large sliced carrots along with the potatoes to this one-pot warmer.

MAKES 4 SERVINGS

PER SERVING

calories	435
protein	15 g
fat	24 g
carbohydrate	41 g
source of fibre	high
source of iron	good

Knackwurst and Cabbage One-Pot Supper

This steaming pot of spicy, plump knackwurst with cabbage and potatoes is sheer winter comfort food. Serve with mustard pickles or hot mustard.

4	Knackwurst sausages (12 oz/375 g)	4
4	Red-skinned potatoes, halved	4
2	Onions, sliced	2
6 cups	Shredded cabbage	1.5 L
3/4 tsp	Caraway seeds	4 mL

1. Prick knackwurst; arrange in large Dutch oven or heavy saucepan. Top with potatoes, onions and cabbage. Sprinkle with caraway seeds and 1/2 tsp (2 mL) each salt and pepper.

2. Add 3/4 cup (175 mL) water; bring to boil over medium-high heat. Reduce heat to low; cover and simmer for 1 hour or until vegetables are tender.

3. Toss gently to mix; simmer, uncovered, for about 10 minutes or until almost all liquid is evaporated.

Pork and Squash Skillet Supper

Orange is considered an appetizing color. Perhaps that's one reason why this supper is such a favorite. It's also quick and easy — and tasty with its twist of frisky fresh citrus.

1	Acorn squash	1
2	Oranges	2
4	Boneless pork loin chops (1 lb/500 g total)	4
½ tsp	Dried thyme	2 mL
2 tbsp	Packed brown sugar	25 mL

1. Cut squash in half lengthwise; scoop out seeds with large spoon. Place flat side down; cut crosswise into ³/₄-inch (2 cm) thick crescents. Set aside.

2. With zester, scrape off outer rind from 1 of the oranges; squeeze and strain juice. Cut remaining orange in half lengthwise; cut crosswise into thin slices. Set aside.

3. Trim any fat from chops; rub with thyme and ¹/₄ tsp (1 mL) each salt and pepper. In large nonstick skillet, heat 2 tsp (10 mL) vegetable oil over medium–high heat; brown chops on both sides, about 5 minutes. Transfer to plate.

4. Drain off any fat in skillet; reduce heat to medium. Add 1 tbsp (15 mL) water, stirring to scrape up any brown bits. Add squash in single layer; sprinkle with orange rind and juice and brown sugar. Cover and cook for 10 minutes or until almost fork-tender.

5. Turn squash over and arrange around edge of skillet; place chops in centre. Cover and cook for about 8 minutes or until squash is tender and juices run clear when pork is pierced and just a hint of pink remains inside. Serve with reserved orange slices.

Salsa Beef Brisket

Nothing is more "fast-fix" than a beef brisket, but it does take considerable roasting time for this lean fibrous cut to turn into the fork-tender treat that will have everyone coming back for more.

2	Onions, sliced	2
1-1/2 cups	Medium salsa	375 mL
1/3 cup	Packed brown sugar	75 mL
2 tbsp	Worcestershire sauce	25 mL
1	Beef brisket (4 lb/2 kg), preferably double brisket	1

1. In skillet, heat 2 tsp (10 mL) vegetable oil over medium heat; cook onions, stirring often, for 8 minutes or until softened.

2. Stir in salsa, sugar, Worcestershire sauce and 1/2 tsp (2 mL) pepper; cook for 5 minutes, stirring occasionally. Let cool.

3. Place brisket in shallow roasting pan or baking dish. Pour salsa mixture over top; turn to coat both sides. Cover and marinate in refrigerator for at least 4 hours or for up to 24 hours, turning occasionally.

4. Cover with lid or foil; roast in 325°F (160°C) oven, basting 3 or 4 times with pan juices, for 3 to 3-1/2 hours or until fork-tender.

5. Uncover and roast for 20 minutes to brown brisket and evaporate some of the juices. Transfer to cutting board; tent with foil and let rest for 10 minutes before slicing thinly across the grain.

6. Meanwhile, skim all visible fat from pan juices; heat to steaming. Serve with beef.

Dairy

Dairy

Dairy TIPS

- *Four ounces (125 g) of firm, semifirm or semisoft cheese usually equals about 1 cup (250 mL) shredded cheese.*

- *To determine lower-fat cheeses, look for the percentage of butterfat (B.F.) or milk fat (M.F.) on labels. Lower-fat, or light, cheeses range from 2 to 20%.*

- *To avoid stringy or rubbery cheese when used in cooking, shred or cut it into small pieces and stir it into the sauce or other mixture toward the end of cooking time, stirring just until it melts.*

- *Check package dates on fresh cheeses such as cottage cheese, cream cheese and ricotta, because they are highly perishable.*

- *A vegetable peeler or cheese plane makes quick work of shaving off thin strips or slivers of cheese for salads and garnishes.*

- *Choose lower-fat dairy products whenever possible. Milk, sour cream, yogurt, cottage cheese, ricotta and cream cheese all come in lower-fat versions, and for the most part, these lighter versions work just as well in cooking as the regular ones.*

- *Be aware of amounts of lower-fat dairy products, especially cheese. It makes no sense to pile on lower-fat products to get the same taste you would get with a smaller amount of a higher-fat but fuller-flavored product. It is often better to choose robust cheeses, such as Parmesan, an old or extra-old Cheddar or zesty feta, in small amounts rather than a milder, lighter cheese such as part-skim mozzarella.*

▼ RICOTTA ALFREDO WITH BROCCOLI
(RECIPE, PAGE 49)

MENU

Cheddar Cheese Noodle
Pudding

Watercress and Endive Salad
with Sliced Oranges

TIP

Since we eat with our eyes first, choose an orange-colored Cheddar cheese.

•

This is an ideal pantry-ready dish. Eggs, cheese and light sour cream are staples in the refrigerator, and egg noodles are ready to cook whenever you are.

Cheddar Cheese Noodle Pudding

Rich! Yes, and very special occasion, this traditional Jewish dairy dish is lightened with beaten egg whites. A deeply satisfying dish, this makes an easy pleasing supper from staples you can keep on hand.

1	Pkg (12 oz/375 g) broad egg noodles	1
3	Eggs, separated	3
2 cups	Shredded old or extra-old Cheddar cheese	500 mL
1 cup	Light sour cream	250 mL
3 tbsp	Butter, melted	50 mL

1. In large pot of lightly salted boiling water, cook noodles for 8 to 10 minutes or until tender but firm. Drain well and transfer to large bowl.

2. Add egg yolks, Cheddar cheese, sour cream, butter and 1/4 tsp (1 mL) each salt and pepper; mix well.

3. In separate bowl, beat egg whites until soft peaks form; fold half into noodle mixture. Scrape into lightly greased 11- by 7-inch (2 L) baking dish. Spread remaining egg whites over top.

4. Bake in 350°F (180°C) oven for about 45 minutes or until golden brown. Serve hot or warm.

MAKES 6 SERVINGS

PER SERVING	
calories	505
protein	23 g
fat	25 g
carbohydrate	46 g
source of fibre	high
source of calcium	excellent

step by step

Add pasta to boiling salted water; cook for 8 minutes.

Meanwhile, in food processor, purée ricotta and milk until very smooth.

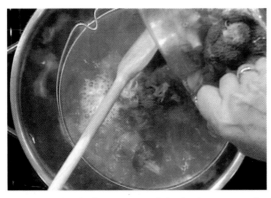

Add broccoli to boiling pasta; cook for 2 minutes or until pasta is tender but still firm to the bite.

Reserving some of the cooking liquid, drain pasta and broccoli well.

Toss pasta and broccoli with sauce.

Sprinkle with Parmesan cheese to serve.

TIP

Frozen broccoli can replace the fresh. Add to pasta for only the last minute of cooking. Other frozen vegetables such as peas, or quick-cooking fresh vegetables such as spinach or grated zucchini, can be added instead — again for only the last minute of cooking.

•

Keep in mind that you shouldn't add oil to pasta when it's boiling, nor rinse it once it's cooked. The oil is not necessary to prevent pasta from sticking together if you use plenty of water and a big pot. As for the rinsing, sauce won't stick to the pasta if it has been rinsed.

MAKES 4 SERVINGS

PER SERVING

calories	470
protein	25 g
fat	9 g
carbohydrate	71 g
source of fibre	high
source of calcium	excellent

Ricotta Alfredo with Broccoli

Certain dishes catch on. Rich, buttery, cheesy fettuccine Alfredo can be counted among the ones with the widest possible appeal. For this lighter Monday-to-Friday version, let ricotta cheese take over from higher-fat whipping cream and butter in the original. And just to make sure vegetables don't get forgotten, there's a goodly amount of broccoli to simmer efficiently with the pasta.

12 oz	Fettuccine pasta	375 g
4 cups	Broccoli florets	1 L
1 cup	Light ricotta cheese	250 mL
1/2 cup	Milk	125 mL
1/2 cup	Freshly grated Parmesan cheese	125 mL

1. In large pot of boiling salted water, cook fettuccine for 8 minutes. Stir in broccoli; cook for 2 minutes or until tender and pasta is tender but still firm to the bite. Drain well in colander, reserving 1/2 cup (125 mL) of the cooking water.

2. Return pasta mixture and reserved cooking liquid to pot over medium heat.

3. Meanwhile, in food processor, purée ricotta with milk until very smooth. Blend in 1/4 tsp (1 mL) each salt and pepper.

4. Scrape cheese mixture over pasta mixture; cook, stirring and lifting pasta constantly, for about 1 minute or until well coated. Sprinkle with Parmesan cheese to serve.

Quick Croque Monsieur

Ham and cheese sandwiches, French-style, are one of those all-day dishes for everyday yet for special occasions, too.

2	**Eggs**	2
1-1/4 cups	**Milk**	300 mL
2 tbsp	**Sweet mustard**	25 mL
8	**Slices egg bread**	8
4	**Slices Swiss cheese**	4

1. In large pie plate, whisk together eggs, milk and 1/4 tsp (1 mL) each salt and pepper; set aside.

2. Spread mustard evenly over 1 side of each bread slice. Top 4 of the slices with cheese; sandwich with remaining bread slices, mustard side down.

3. Dip sandwiches into egg mixture, turning to soak up mixture well. *(Sandwiches can be prepared to this point, covered and refrigerated for up to 2 hours.)*

4. In large nonstick skillet or griddle, heat 1 tsp (5 mL) vegetable oil over medium heat; cook sandwiches, turning once, for about 12 minutes or until golden and crispy, and cheese is melted.

M<small>AKES</small> 4 <small>SERVINGS</small>

PER SERVING	
calories	405
protein	18 g
fat	21 g
carbohydrate	34 g
source of calcium	excellent

Barbecue

Barbecue

Barbecue TIPS

- *Let meat stand for 30 minutes at room temperature before grilling.*

- *When barbecuing a steak or other meat, turn it with tongs instead of a fork to prevent piercing the meat and losing juices.*

- *Check foods often when barbecuing because temperatures can vary widely due to wind and weather conditions.*

- *Trim excess fat from meats to prevent flare-ups. Always keep a spray bottle of water beside the barbecue to extinguish any flare-ups.*

- *Baste with a tomato or sugar-based sauce during only the last 15 minutes of barbecuing, to prevent scorching.*

- *Some marinades are suitable for serving with grilled meat, poultry or fish. Check the recipe for this recommendation. When marinades that have flavored and tenderized raw meat, poultry or fish are to be used as a sauce as well, they must be brought to a boil and boiled for 2 minutes. Strain and serve.*

- *Cover cooked meat (except burgers) with foil and let rest for 5 minutes after cooking to allow the juices to redistribute throughout the meat.*

- *Cut less-tender steaks across the grain to add to their tenderness.*

- *Bring a clean plate to the barbecue for cooked meats. Never put them back on plates that have held raw meat or chicken.*

- *Wood chips, such as mesquite or hickory, added to the barbecue's rocks or coals lend a smoky flavor to food. Soak the chips in hot water for 30 minutes before adding to the barbecue.*

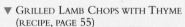

▼ GRILLED LAMB CHOPS WITH THYME
(RECIPE, PAGE 55)

MENU

Really Good Flank Steak

Mashed Potatoes

Broccoli Florets

TIP

You can tuck thin slices of the meat into tortillas along with shredded romaine lettuce, sliced avocado and fresh tomato salsa.

Really Good Flank Steak

Authentic Worcestershire sauce — with its mellow blend of onions, garlic, tamarind, vinegar and anchovies (among a host of other ingredients in the secret formula) — adds robust flavor to any marinade. Here, it bolsters the good beef flavor of lean flank steak.

2	Cloves garlic, minced	2
3 tbsp	Red wine vinegar	50 mL
1 tbsp	Worcestershire sauce	15 mL
1 tbsp	Dijon mustard	15 mL
1	Flank steak (1–¹/₂ lb/750 g)	1

1. In shallow glass dish, stir together garlic, vinegar, 2 tbsp (25 mL) vegetable oil, Worcestershire sauce, mustard and ¹/₄ tsp (1 mL) pepper.

2. Lay steak in marinade; turn to coat all over. Cover and marinate in refrigerator for at least 4 hours or for up to 24 hours, turning a few times. Let stand at room temperature for 30 minutes before cooking.

3. Reserving marinade, place steak on greased grill or broiler rack. Close lid and grill, brushing with reserved marinade several times, for about 4 minutes per side for rare or to desired doneness.

4. Using tongs, transfer steak to cutting board. Tent with foil and let stand for about 5 minutes. Slice thinly across the grain.

MAKES 6 SERVINGS

PER SERVING	
calories	240
protein	26 g
fat	13 g
carbohydrate	1 g

Is It Done Yet?

Try using your fingers in a touch test to determine how your steaks are progressing: if the steak is soft to the touch, it is rare; if it springs back when touched, it is medium; if it is firm, it is well done. Another test for doneness is to use the tip of a pointed sharp knife to slit the steak or the chop to see the color inside and adjust cooking times accordingly. But keep in mind that the heat in the meat or fish will keep it cooking after it is taken off the grill.

step by step

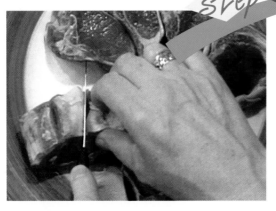

Trim fat from chops to 1/4-inch (5 mm) thickness; slash remaining fat at 1-inch (2.5 cm) intervals.

For marinade, whisk together wine, oil, vinegar, thyme, anchovy paste, pepper, and salt if desired.

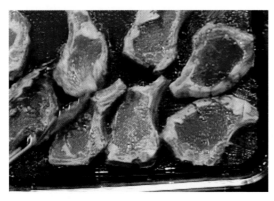

Pour marinade over chops; turn chops to coat well. Cover and marinate.

Reserving marinade, place chops on greased grill over medium-high heat.

Grill, brushing with marinade, for about 7 minutes per side for medium-rare.

Touch test for doneness: If surface is springy, chops are rare to medium-rare.

MENU

Grilled Lamb Chops with Thyme

Garlic-Roasted Mashed Potatoes

Ratatouille

TIP

This feisty marinade adds a new dimension to thick boneless or bone-in pork chops as well.

•

You can replace the anchovy paste with chopped drained canned anchovies. Count on about 1 anchovy per 1 tsp (5 mL).

Grilled Lamb Chops with Thyme

The gutsy flavors of Provence take a turn as inspiration for these perfectly grilled lamb chops.

8	**Loin lamb chops** (1-$^1/_2$ lb/750 g total)	8
$^1/_4$ cup	**Red wine**	50 mL
2 tsp	**Red wine vinegar**	10 mL
1 tsp	**Dried thyme**	5 mL
1 tsp	**Anchovy paste**	5 mL

1. Trim fat from chops to $^1/_4$-inch (5 mm) thickness; slash remaining fat at 1-inch (2.5 cm) intervals. Place in shallow glass dish.

2. In small dish, whisk together wine, 1 tbsp (15 mL) olive oil, vinegar, thyme, anchovy paste, $^1/_2$ tsp (2 mL) pepper, and pinch salt if desired.

3. Pour marinade over chops, turning to coat well. Cover with plastic wrap. Marinate at room temperature for 30 minutes or in refrigerator for up to 8 hours. Remove from refrigerator 30 minutes before cooking.

4. Reserving any marinade, place lamb on greased grill over medium-high heat; close lid and grill, brushing with any marinade, for about 7 minutes per side for medium-rare or until desired doneness.

MAKES 4 SERVINGS

PER SERVING	
calories	175
protein	11 g
fat	14 g
carbohydrate	1 g

Roasted Garlic

You can roast garlic ahead of time and add it to mashed potatoes or a salad dressing. When the oven is on for another dish, loosely enclose 8 to 10 unpeeled cloves in foil. Roast at 350°F (180°C) for about 30 minutes or until very tender to the touch. Let cool. (Refrigerate the cloves you don't need immediately.) To use, simply press the pointed end of the garlic and the roasted clove pops out the wide end. Mash before adding to potatoes or dressings.

MENU

Grilled Chicken with Lemon
and Garlic

Grilled Potatoes

Summer-Roasted Vegetables

TIP

To roast instead of grill chicken, marinate and place, meaty side down, in shallow roasting pan. Bake in 375°F (190°C) oven for about 45 minutes, turning once.

•

For a complete meal, serve with grilled vegetables: Halve sweet or white potatoes, brush lightly with oil and place on the grill at the same time as the chicken. Round out a summer-kissed meal with other vegetables, such as thickly sliced zucchini, onion slices and quartered sweet red, green and yellow peppers, which need less time to cook than the potatoes, about 20 minutes.

MAKES 4 SERVINGS

PER SERVING	
calories	290
protein	30 g
fat	17 g
carbohydrate	2 g

Grilled Chicken with Lemon and Garlic

Simplicity is the key word when it comes to chicken. Nothing is finer with the bird than a drizzle of good olive oil, the zing of lemon and some garlic that lets you know it's there. But go ahead and add whatever else you fancy — hot pepper flakes for a piri piri touch, oregano and/or mint for a Greek flair or rosemary for a more restrained flavor. Another variation is simply to grate in even more pepper, using mixed peppercorns if desired.

2	Large lemons	2
4	Cloves garlic, minced	4
1/4 tsp	Hot pepper flakes	1 mL
Pinch	Dried oregano	Pinch
2 lb	Chicken legs	1 kg

1. With zester or grater, remove yellow rind from 1-1/2 of the lemons; place in shallow glass dish. Squeeze and strain juice into dish.

2. Add 2 tbsp (25 mL) extra-virgin olive oil, garlic, hot pepper flakes, oregano and pinch each salt and pepper. Add chicken, turning to coat well.

3. Cover and marinate in refrigerator for at least 4 hours or for up to 24 hours, turning a few times. Let stand at room temperature for 30 minutes before grilling.

4. Reserving marinade, place chicken, meaty side down, on greased grill; close lid and cook, brushing with marinade and turning every 10 minutes, for 30 to 40 minutes or until juices run clear when chicken is pierced.

5. Cut remaining lemon half into wedges to garnish or squeeze over chicken.

Vegetarian

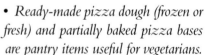

Vegetarian

RECULES

RECIPES

▼ QUESADILLA TORTE
   (RECIPE, PAGE 61)

Vegetarian TIPS

- *Leaving the skin on vegetables and fruits gives you a bonus of fibre and nutrition.*

- *If root vegetables such as beets and carrots have their leaves attached, remove them as soon as possible to prevent the greens from leaching moisture from the vegetable.*

- *Limp vegetables such as carrots and celery regain some of their crisp texture if soaked in ice water.*

- *Save any liquid used for cooking vegetables for use in soups, stews and sauces.*

- *For quick suppers, look to canned beans, chick-peas and lentils. Drain, rinse and add them to pasta dishes, salads, vegetables and rice.*

- *Ready-made pizza dough (frozen or fresh) and partially baked pizza bases are pantry items useful for vegetarians.*

- *Hummus or bean spreads are great ingredients for sandwiches. Just add sprouts, sliced tomatoes and cucumbers.*

- *Tofu, especially tofu with calcium sulphate in the list of ingredients, is great for a variety of quick vegetarian meals. Cube tofu and add to vegetable-rich broths. Cube a firm tofu to add to stir-fries. Grate firm tofu to serve as a garnish for soups, in a salad or with pasta. Marinate pieces of tofu overnight in Asian flavors and grill. Crumble tofu into a ratatouille as it finishes bubbling on the stove or add it to a chili made without meat.*

MENU

Potato Torte with Mushrooms

Steamed Green Beans

Fresh Tomato Salad with Basil and Balsamic Dressing

TIP

Add a sprinkle of dried or fresh thyme or rosemary to the onions and mushrooms.

•

To test the heat of the interior of this casserole and others, especially ones you're reheating, insert tip of pointed knife into centre of casserole for a few seconds. Immediately test the knife's temperature by touching with finger or back of wrist. Be careful not to burn yourself.

MAKES 6 SERVINGS

PER SERVING	
calories	290
protein	10 g
fat	12 g
carbohydrate	38 g
source of fibre	high
source of calcium	good

Potato Torte with Mushrooms

Layer potatoes with golden onions, mushrooms and a sprinkle of cheese for a new version of a potato cake.

6	Potatoes (2-½ lb/1.25 kg)	6
¼ cup	Butter	50 mL
1	Large red onion, chopped	1
6 cups	Sliced mushrooms (1 lb/500 g)	1.5 L
1 cup	Shredded light Cheddar-style cheese	250 mL

1. Scrub potatoes. In large pot of boiling salted water, cover and cook potatoes for 25 minutes or just until tender. Drain and return to pot to heat for a few seconds to dry. Let cool enough to handle. Peel if desired; cut into scant ¼-inch (5 mm) thick slices.

2. Meanwhile, in large skillet, melt butter over medium heat; cook onion, mushrooms and ½ tsp (2 mL) pepper, stirring often, for 10 to 15 minutes or until liquid is evaporated and onions are golden.

3. Arrange half of the potatoes in overlapping circles in greased 9- or 10-inch (23 or 25 cm) springform pan. Sprinkle with ¼ tsp (1 mL) salt. Top with mushroom mixture and half of the cheese. Arrange remaining potatoes in overlapping circles over top.

4. Add ½ cup (125 mL) water to skillet; bring to boil, stirring to scrape up brown bits from bottom of pan. Boil for 1 minute or until reduced slightly. Drizzle over potatoes. Sprinkle with remaining cheese.

5. Bake in 350°F (180°C) oven for about 25 minutes or until golden and crusty and centre is steaming. Let stand for 10 minutes; unmould and cut into wedges.

step by step

Cook onions in vegetable oil until softened.

Add beans, water and pepper; cover and cook over low heat until warmed through.

Place 1 of the tortillas in springform pan; spread with one-third of the bean mixture, then one-third of the salsa.

Sprinkle with some of the cheese, then repeat layers twice.

Cut remaining tortilla into wedges. Arrange in original shape on top.

Bake until torte is golden brown and cheese is melted. Let cool slightly before slicing.

MAKES 6 TO 8 SERVINGS

PER 8 SERVINGS	
calories	355
protein	18 g
fat	12 g
carbohydrate	44 g
source of fibre	very high
source of calcium	good
source of iron	excellent

Quesadilla Torte

Tortillas layered with a savory bean mixture, salsa and cheese are an easy vegetarian supper. The bonus? Most of the ingredients are pantry-handy.

2	Onions, chopped	2
2	Cans (each 19 oz/540 mL) black or red kidney beans or romano beans	2
1-³/₄ cups	Shredded Cheddar or Monterey Jack cheese	425 mL
4	10-inch (25 cm) flour tortillas	4
1-¹/₂ cups	Chunky salsa	375 mL

1. In skillet, heat 1 tbsp (15 mL) vegetable oil over medium heat; cook onions, stirring occasionally, for 5 minutes or until softened.

2. Drain and rinse beans; add to pan. Add ¹/₂ cup (125 mL) water and ¹/₄ tsp (1 mL) pepper; cover and cook over low heat for about 5 minutes or until beans are heated through and water is absorbed. Let cool slightly.

3. Set ¹/₄ cup (50 mL) of the cheese aside. Place 1 of the tortillas in 10-inch (25 cm) springform pan. Spread with one-third of the bean mixture, one-third of the salsa and one-third of the remaining cheese. Repeat layers twice. Cut remaining tortilla into 6 to 8 wedges; arrange in original round shape on top. Brush with ¹/₂ tsp (2 mL) vegetable oil. Sprinkle with reserved cheese.

4. Bake in 400°F (200°C) oven for 20 to 25 minutes or until crisp and golden, cheese is melted and beans are heated through. Let cool slightly before removing side of pan and cutting into 6 to 8 wedges to serve.

MENU

Stuffed Eggplant

Endive Spears with Tzatziki Dressing

Warm Focaccia

TIP

When cooking eggplant, remember that it is one of the vegetables that should always be thoroughly cooked and soft. This brings out its creaminess and best flavor.

•

Extra-virgin olive oil, the green or yellow one with a peppery nose, will boost flavors in this eggplant dish.

Stuffed Eggplant

Roasted eggplants team up with tomatoes to make you think of summer even on the coldest, darkest days of the year.

2	Eggplants (12 oz/375 g each)	2
2	Onions, chopped	2
4	Cloves garlic, slivered	4
1 tsp	Dried thyme	5 mL
2 cups	Chopped canned tomatoes	500 mL

1. Cut each eggplant in half lengthwise; trim off stems. With spoon, scoop out flesh, leaving ½-inch (1 cm) thick shell. Sprinkle inside with 2 tsp (10 mL) salt; let drain, cut side down, in colander in sink. Chop flesh; sprinkle with ½ tsp (2 mL) salt. Add to colander; let stand for 30 minutes. Rinse and press dry in towels.

2. Meanwhile, in large skillet, heat 2 tbsp (25 mL) extra-virgin olive oil over medium heat; cook onions and garlic, stirring occasionally, for about 10 minutes or until very soft and beginning to turn golden. Add thyme and chopped eggplant; cook for about 10 minutes or until eggplant is translucent.

3. Stir in tomatoes; cook, stirring often, for about 5 minutes or until moisture is evaporated. Season with ¼ tsp (1 mL) pepper.

4. Wipe out interior of eggplant shells. Place in shallow baking dish or roasting pan. Fill with tomato mixture. Drizzle with 1 tsp (5 mL) extra-virgin olive oil.

5. Cover and bake in 350°F (180°C) oven for 30 minutes. Uncover and bake for 10 minutes longer or until stuffing is lightly crusted and eggplant and shell are very tender but shell is not collapsed.

MAKES 4 SERVINGS

PER SERVING	
calories	165
protein	3 g
fat	9 g
carbohydrate	22 g
source of fibre	very high

MENU

Bean Burgers with Coriander Cream on Whole Wheat Kaisers

Corn on the Cob

TIP

Patties can be made up to several hours ahead, covered and refrigerated. Likewise, the coriander cream mixture can wait with grace for up to 4 hours.

•

You can substitute black or romano beans for the red kidney beans.

Bean Burgers with Coriander Cream

When it comes to cooking for a vegetarian and burgers are on the menu, nothing is easier than these bean-based patties. Experiment with all sorts of toppings, such as diced avocado, a generous mound of shredded romaine lettuce or sprouts or a little cheese such as Monterey Jack or creamy fontina. Mild or medium salsa is plenty hot for most people, especially when salsa is not just a condiment but the central ingredient that adds moisture and flavor to the patties.

1	Can (19 oz/540 mL) red kidney beans	1
1/2 cup	Dry bread crumbs	125 mL
1/2 cup	Salsa	125 mL
1/3 cup	Light sour cream	75 mL
2 tbsp	Minced fresh coriander	25 mL

1. Drain and rinse beans; place in bowl. With potato masher or fork, mash beans until fairly smooth but still with some small lumps.

2. Stir in bread crumbs and salsa to make fairly firm mixture. With wet hands, form into four 1/2-inch (1 cm) thick patties; set aside on waxed paper.

3. In small bowl, stir together sour cream and coriander.

4. In large nonstick skillet, heat 2 tsp (10 mL) vegetable oil over medium–high heat; cook patties, turning once, for 10 minutes or until crusty outside and piping hot inside. Serve topped with coriander cream.

MAKES 4 SERVINGS

PER SERVING	
calories	220
protein	11 g
fat	4 g
carbohydrate	34 g
source of fibre	very high

*Couscous-Stuffed
Acorn Squash*

*Spinach and Red Cabbage
Salad*

TIP

Quick-cooking couscous
is processed wheat and is
available in bulk- and health-
food stores, Middle Eastern
groceries and some
supermarkets.

•

Vary the vegetables in the
couscous stuffing. Choose fresh
vegetables in season, or try
frozen peas and beans.

•

The corn can be frozen or
drained canned kernels.

MAKES 4 SERVINGS

PER SERVING	
calories	390
protein	11 g
fat	3 g
carbohydrate	87 g
source of fibre	very high
source of calcium	good
source of iron	excellent

Couscous-Stuffed Acorn Squash

*If there are boots made for walking, there are vegetables
made for stuffing. The star of the stuffable vegetables is
squash, especially acorn or pepper squash.*

2	**Acorn squash (4 lb/2 kg total)**	2
3/4 **cup**	**Couscous**	**175 mL**
1	**Onion, chopped**	1
1	**Can (19 oz/540 mL) stewed tomatoes**	1
1-1/2 **cups**	**Corn kernels**	**375 mL**

1. Halve and seed squash. Cut 1/2-inch (1 cm) thick
   slice from each cut side; peel and dice. Set diced
   squash aside.

2. Place squash halves, cut side down, on lightly
   greased baking sheet. Bake in 400°F (200°C) oven
   for 40 to 45 minutes or until very tender.

3. Meanwhile, in saucepan, bring 1 cup (250 mL)
   water to boil. Stir in couscous. Cover and remove
   from heat; let stand for 5 minutes. Fluff with fork.

4. In separate saucepan, heat 2 tsp (10 mL) vegetable oil
   over medium heat; cook onion, stirring occasionally,
   for 5 minutes or until softened and golden.

5. Stir in tomatoes and reserved squash; bring to boil.
   Reduce heat and simmer for 20 to 25 minutes or
   until thickened. Remove from heat. Stir in corn and
   couscous; season with pinch each salt and pepper.

6. Turn squash cut side up on baking sheet; spoon
   stuffing into each half. Cover with foil; bake for
   10 minutes or until filling is hot.

Salads

Salads

Salad TIPS

- *Always dress salads at the last possible moment, using the least amount of salad dressing possible.*

- *Lighten mayonnaise-based dressing with low-fat yogurt or buttermilk.*

- *You can lower the amount of oil needed in a dressing not simply by increasing the amount of vinegar but by balancing out the acidity with the addition of some stock or wine, a fruit juice such as apple, or even water.*

- *Side salads can easily be turned into main-course salads with the addition of sliced hard-cooked eggs, cubed or shredded cheese, tofu or drained, rinsed cooked legumes.*

- *Keep a supply of carrots, broccoli stalks and celery on hand for quick crisper crudités. They can take the place of a side salad, and kids especially like to dip them into a light, clingy salad dressing, such as a ranch-type dressing (see Dilly Ranch, page 72).*

- *When the crisper drawer begins to look a little empty, keep shredded carrots in mind for a quick salad to dress with lemon juice, parsley, salt, pepper and a drizzle of canola oil.*

- *Ready-mixed salad greens are now available in most supermarkets. Although more expensive than greens you clean and mix, they offer excellent variety and there is no waste or preparation time.*

▼ GRILLED CHICKEN AND SPINACH
SALAD WITH GARLIC CROÛTES
(RECIPE, PAGE 69)

MENU

Pasta with Pesto and Tomatoes

Italian Bread and Ripe
Black Olives

TIP

This thick flavorful sauce is generally not moist enough to coat a pasta salad without additional lashings of oil or other high-calorie items. Tossing it with some of the cooking liquid adds moisture without fat.

•

Pasta for salad can be rinsed briefly in colander under cold water; shake colander to drain well.

MAKES 4 SERVINGS

PER SERVING	
calories	445
protein	16 g
fat	12 g
carbohydrate	68 g
source of fibre	high

Pasta with Pesto and Tomatoes

Summer comes and goes, and just as there are never enough hot days to satisfy a vacationer, there is never enough basil for cooks hooked on the Mediterranean flavors of pesto. Reawaken memories of those relaxed days and bold warm-weather flavors with an easy pesto pasta salad that calls on bottled basil pesto for that special hit. You can add diced sweet red peppers and, if you like, a scattering of chopped red onion.

4-1/2 cups	Fusilli pasta (12 oz/375 g)	1.125 L
1/3 cup	Bottled pesto	75 mL
2	Tomatoes, diced	2
1/2 cup	Diced sweet yellow pepper	125 mL
1/4 cup	Freshly grated Parmesan cheese (approx)	50 mL

1. In large pot of boiling salted water, cook pasta for 8 to 10 minutes or until tender but still firm. Drain in colander, reserving 1/2 cup (125 mL) of the cooking water; rinse with cold water.

2. Dump pasta into large pasta bowl. Add pesto and about 1/4 cup (50 mL) of the reserved cooking liquid; toss gently to coat evenly. Let cool.

3. Add tomatoes, yellow pepper, Parmesan, and a bit more cooking liquid if desired; toss again gently. Sprinkle with more cheese, if desired, and 1/4 tsp (1 mL) pepper.

step by step

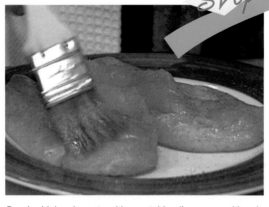

Brush chicken breasts with vegetable oil; season with salt and pepper.

Grill chicken until no longer pink inside. Let cool slightly; cut across the grain into thin slices.

For dressing, whisk together 1 minced garlic clove, olive oil, vinegar, salt and pepper.

For croûtes, brush bread with olive oil on both sides. Toast in oven until golden brown. Halve remaining garlic lengthwise and rub on 1 side of croûtes.

Arrange spinach in bowl; top with chicken slices. Drizzle with dressing; toss to coat.

Arrange croûtes around side of bowl.

MENU

Grilled Chicken and Spinach Salad with Garlic Croûtes

Cantaloupe and Honeydew Slices with Ginger

TIP

Chicken can be prepared up to 1 day ahead and refrigerated. Garlic croûtes are best freshly made.

•

Garlic often has a green sprout, especially in the spring when it is about to grow. Halve the garlic and, with the tip of a pointed knife, lift out and discard this harsh part.

MAKES 4 SERVINGS

PER SERVING	
calories	470
protein	23 g
fat	26 g
carbohydrate	37 g
source of fibre	high
source of calcium	good
source of iron	excellent

Grilled Chicken and Spinach Salad with Garlic Croûtes

When making a main-course salad that depends on greens as a base, choose greens with oomph. Spinach is always available and a good pick, but look also for tender hearts of curly endive or escarole, or a mix of greens.

2	Boneless skinless chicken breasts	2
2	Large cloves garlic	2
2 tbsp	Red wine vinegar	25 mL
8	Slices French baguette	8
10 cups	Trimmed fresh spinach	2.5 L

1. Brush chicken with 2 tsp (10 mL) vegetable oil; sprinkle with ¼ tsp (1 mL) pepper and pinch salt. Cook in grill pan or in skillet over medium heat, turning once, for 8 to 10 minutes or until no longer pink inside. Let cool slightly; cut across the grain into thin slices. Set aside.

2. Meanwhile, mince 1 of the garlic cloves; place in small bowl. Add ¼ cup (50 mL) extra-virgin olive oil, vinegar and ¼ tsp (1 mL) each salt and pepper; whisk until blended. Set aside.

3. Brush both sides of bread with 2 tbsp (25 mL) extra-virgin olive oil; toast on baking sheet in 375°F (190°C) oven, turning once, for about 10 minutes or until golden.

4. Halve remaining garlic lengthwise; immediately rub over 1 side of toast.

5. Arrange spinach in salad bowl; scatter chicken over top. Drizzle with dressing; toss to coat. Arrange croûtes around side of bowl.

MENU

White Bean and Tuna Salad

Multigrain Rolls

TIP

The salad can be covered and refrigerated for up to 8 hours ahead of time. You can also wash and spin-dry the lettuce beforehand.

•

Vary the salad with drained red sockeye salmon, skin removed, instead of the tuna. You can substitute other beans, too, depending on what you have on hand.

MAKES 3 SERVINGS

PER SERVING	
calories	400
protein	28 g
fat	12 g
carbohydrate	47 g
source of fibre	very high
source of iron	excellent

White Bean and Tuna Salad

With a can of beans and tuna stocked in the cupboard, the call to come and sit down to an absolutely delicious salad supper is only five minutes away.

1	Can (19 oz/540 mL) navy (white pea) beans	1
1	Can (6.5 oz/184 g) water-packed chunk white tuna	1
1	Small red onion or sweet green pepper, finely chopped	1
1	Jar (6.5 oz/192 mL) marinated artichoke hearts	1
1	Head Boston or Bibb lettuce, separated	1

1. Drain and rinse beans. Drain tuna; break into bite-size pieces. In bowl, toss together beans, tuna and red onion.

2. Drain artichoke hearts, pouring marinade over bean mixture. Cut hearts into quarters; add to beans. Season with 1/4 tsp (1 mL) salt and pinch pepper; toss gently.

3. Line salad plates or shallow bowls with lettuce leaves; spoon in salad.

Lettuce Care

To prepare and store lettuce, it is important to have it moist but not wet. Separate lettuce leaves, rinse them in a basin of cold water and spin-dry in a salad spinner. Arrange the leaves in a single layer on a tea towel; roll up the towel loosely and enclose in plastic bag. Store in refrigerator. The towel is important because it absorbs excess moisture and prevents the formation of the weeknight cook's enemy — crisper slime.

Steak and Potato Salad with Horseradish Vinaigrette

Here is the best of the basics: chunky potatoes with slices of deli or leftover beef (either grilled steak or from a roast) tossed in a memorable dressing. Feel free — when time and provisions allow — for a few add-ins: chopped sweet green or red pepper, celery or cucumber, watercress or fresh herbs such as chives or parsley.

2 lb	Small red potatoes (6 to 8)	1 kg
¼ cup	White wine vinegar or cider vinegar	50 mL
4 tsp	Dijon mustard with horseradish	20 mL
1-½ cups	Strips cooked beef	375 mL
4	Green onions, sliced	4

1. Scrub potatoes. In pot of boiling salted water, cover and cook potatoes for about 20 minutes or until fork-tender. Drain and return to pot to dry for about 30 seconds. Let cool slightly; cut into 1-inch (2.5 cm) cubes. Place in salad bowl.

2. In separate bowl, whisk together ⅓ cup (75 mL) vegetable oil, vinegar, mustard and ¼ tsp (1 mL) each salt and pepper.

3. Drizzle half of the vinaigrette over potatoes; toss gently to coat. Cover and refrigerate for at least 30 minutes or for up to 4 hours.

4. Add beef, green onions and remaining vinaigrette; toss to mix well and coat evenly.

MAKES 4 SERVINGS

PER SERVING	
calories	535
protein	33 g
fat	27 g
carbohydrate	40 g
source of iron	excellent

Handy Salad Dressings

On a busy day after work and school, making a salad may seem like the last thing you want to do. But if the lettuce is washed and waiting and there's a superior homemade dressing in the fridge, chances are you will make a salad. Here are two dressings to have on hand.

CLASSIC OIL AND VINEGAR

1	Clove garlic	1
¼ cup	Vegetable or extra-virgin olive oil	50 mL
2 tbsp	White or red wine vinegar	25 mL
1 tsp	Dijon mustard	5 mL
Pinch	Granulated sugar	Pinch

1. Quarter garlic. On cutting board and using fork, crush garlic with ¼ tsp (1 mL) salt.

2. In jar, shake together garlic, oil, vinegar, mustard and sugar until blended. *(Dressing can be sealed and refrigerated for up to 2 days.)*

DILLY RANCH

¼ cup	Light mayonnaise	50 mL
1 tbsp	White wine vinegar or cider vinegar	15 mL
1 tsp	Dried dillweed	5 mL
1 tsp	Dijon mustard	5 mL
½ cup	Buttermilk	125 mL

1. In jar, stir together mayonnaise, vinegar, dillweed and mustard. Pour in buttermilk; shake to blend. *(Dressing can be sealed and refrigerated for up to 2 days.)*

TIP

Follow the cue of restaurants and serve a small salad as the first course. Since everyone is hungry, they will attack this healthful part of the meal with gusto.

MAKES ½ CUP (125 mL), ENOUGH FOR 8 CUPS (2 L) GREENS

PER TBSP (15 mL)

calories	65
protein	trace
fat	7 g
carbohydrate	trace

MAKES ¾ CUP (175 mL), ENOUGH FOR 12 CUPS (3 L) GREENS

PER TBSP (15 mL)

calories	20
protein	trace
fat	2 g
carbohydrate	1 g

Pizza &
Sandwiches

Pizza &
Sandwiches

▼ ITALIAN SAUSAGE AND PEPPER BRAID
(RECIPE, PAGE 77)

Pizza & Sandwich TIPS

- *Sandwiches for supper take on a whole new look. Choose a variety of breads, whole-grain clearly being a first choice for its value-added nutrition.*

- *Tortillas, pita breads, focaccia, bagels and pizza bases are the newest wrappers for sandwiches. Keep a variety of these interesting breads in the freezer, ready to defrost for a quick meal.*

- *For whole-meal sandwiches, keep a supply of canned food on hand, such as tuna packed in water, salmon, lean ham, sardines and chicken.*

- *Toast buns and bread on the grill, in the oven or toaster to boost their flavor.*

- *Try hummus or tzatziki as a spread for sandwiches. They're lower in fat than mayonnaise, butter and margarine and add lots of moisture and flavor.*

- *Canned or jarred roasted red peppers make quick vegetarian sandwiches. If available, spread the bread or bun with goat's cheese or a light herbed cream cheese and pile on the lettuce and a few chopped black olives.*

- *Use your waffle iron or sandwich maker for hot sandwiches. These appliances turn a simple grilled cheese sandwich into a supper that everyone loves.*

MENU

Fresh Tomato Pizza

Toss of Torn Radicchio and
Romaine with Radishes

TIP

A sprinkle of cornmeal on the pan helps prevent pizza dough from sticking to the pan.

A pizza stone makes a crisp crust. The stone needs to be heated according to manufacturer's instructions before adding the dressed pizza.

Instead of sprinkling cheese over the pizza, you can substitute the same amount of pitted black olives.

MAKES 4 SERVINGS

PER SERVING	
calories	715
protein	22 g
fat	15 g
carbohydrate	125 g
source of fibre	very high
source of calcium	good
source of iron	excellent

Fresh Tomato Pizza

Celebrate summer with a fresh, easy pizza. Bake it on the barbecue or in the oven. Tomatoes must be red, ripe and juicy. You'll need about ¼ cup (50 mL) cornmeal to dust over the pizza pan.

	Herbed Pizza Dough (recipe follows)	
2	Large red onions, sliced	2
1 tsp	Dried oregano or basil	5 mL
4	Plum tomatoes	4
⅓ cup	Freshly grated pecorino or Parmesan cheese	75 mL

1. Punch down dough; roll and stretch to fit 12-inch (30 cm) cornmeal-dusted pizza pan, forming raised edge. Let stand for 10 minutes.

2. Meanwhile, in large skillet, heat 2 tbsp (25 mL) extra-virgin olive oil over medium-high heat; cook onions and oregano, stirring often, for 10 minutes or until softened and golden.

3. Spread onions evenly over pizza crust. Slice tomatoes thinly; arrange over onions. Sprinkle with cheese.

4. Bake on bottom rack of 500°F (260°C) oven for about 12 minutes or until crust is golden and crisp and tomatoes are lightly singed and juicy.

Herbed Pizza Dough

Making your own pizza dough is quick and easy: In food processor, whirl together 4 cups (1 L) all-purpose flour, ¼ cup (50 mL) whole wheat flour, 2 pkg quick-rising (instant) dry yeast (or 2 tbsp/25 mL), ¼ cup (50 mL) finely chopped fresh basil (or 2 tsp/10 mL dried) if desired, and 1 tsp (5 mL) granulated sugar.

With motor running, gradually pour in 1-½ cups (375 mL) very hot water. Add 1 tbsp (15 mL) olive oil; whirl, adding up to 2 tbsp (25 mL) more water if necessary, until dough forms ball. Whirl for 1 minute. Transfer to lightly floured surface; cover and let stand for 15 minutes. Makes enough for one 12-inch (30 cm) pizza crust.

step by step

Add pasta sauce to browned sausage and green peppers.

Scrape sausage mixture into bowl and let cool. Stir in ¼ cup (50 mL) of the cheese.

Roll dough into rectangle; sprinkle some cheese in strip down centre. Top with sausage mixture.

Starting at corner of dough, cut diagonal strips. Repeat on other side in opposite direction.

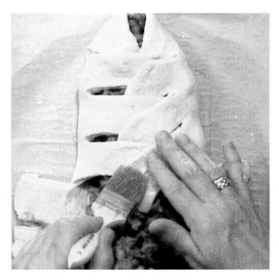

Braid strips over filling to cover, brushing joins with water.

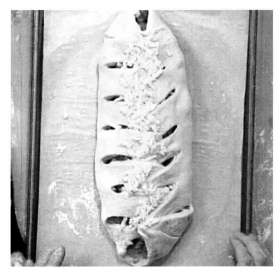

Sprinkle with remaining cheese. Bake until golden.

MENU

Italian Sausage and Pepper Braid

Tossed Leaf Lettuce with Peppercorn Ranch Dressing

VARIATION

Italian Sausage and Pepper Melts: Spread sausage sauce on split Italian or Portuguese loaf. Sprinkle with cheese and broil until bubbling and bread is crisped.

TIP

A tomato pasta sauce with basil, sun-dried tomatoes or mushrooms adds flavor muscle.

You can substitute provolone cheese for the mozzarella and yellow peppers for the green.

MAKES 6 SERVINGS

PER SERVING

calories	495
protein	26 g
fat	21 g
carbohydrate	50 g
source of calcium	good
source of iron	good

Italian Sausage and Pepper Braid

Look for Italian sausage seasoned with fennel.

1 lb	Hot or mild Italian sausages	500 g
2	Sweet green peppers, diced	2
1-¹/₂ cups	Spicy pasta sauce	375 mL
1-¹/₂ cups	Shredded part-skim mozzarella cheese	375 mL
1 lb	Pizza dough	500 g

1. Remove sausages from casings. In greased skillet, brown sausage over medium-high heat, breaking up meat, about 8 minutes. Drain on paper towel-lined plate. Drain fat from pan. Cook green peppers over medium heat, stirring often, for 10 minutes or until browned on edges.

2. Add sausage to pan. Add 1 cup (250 mL) of the pasta sauce; bring to boil. Reduce heat and simmer for 5 minutes or until almost no liquid remains. Scrape into bowl; let cool. Add ¹/₄ cup (50 mL) cheese.

3. On floured surface, roll out dough into 15- by 10-inch (38 by 25 cm) rectangle. Transfer to greased baking sheet. Sprinkle 1 cup (250 mL) of the remaining cheese in 4-inch (10 cm) wide strip lengthwise down centre, leaving 1-inch (2.5 cm) border at top and bottom. Top with sausage mixture.

4. Starting at corner of dough, cut 2-inch (5 cm) wide diagonal strips to within 1 inch (2.5 cm) of filling. Repeat on other side in opposite direction. Braid strips over filling to cover, brushing joins with water. Sprinkle with remaining cheese.

5. Bake in 425°F (220°C) oven for 5 minutes; bake in 400°F (200°C) oven for 20 minutes or until golden. If desired, heat remaining sauce; serve with braid.

MENU

Melts for the Moment

Basket of Cherry Tomatoes
and Celery, Carrot and
Broccoli Sticks

VARIATION

Crab Melt: Substitute canned
or thawed drained crab
for the tuna.

TIP

You can also spread the mixture
over 4 small flour tortillas or
onto split focaccia. Wrap in foil
and bake in 350°F (180°C) oven
for about 15 minutes.

For additional flavor variations,
add ¼ tsp (1 mL) curry
powder or ½ tsp (2 mL) of
any of the following: Italian
herb seasoning, dried basil or
chili powder. In summer, use
fresh herbs, including dill,
basil and parsley.

MAKES 4 SERVINGS

PER SERVING	
calories	500
protein	34 g
fat	21 g
carbohydrate	42 g
source of calcium	good
source of iron	good

Melts for the Moment

*Your freezer, fridge and cupboard can provide you with
plenty of ingredients for quick, hot and satisfying
open-face sandwiches.*

4	**Kaiser or large dinner rolls**	4
2	**Cans (each 7 oz/213 g) water-packed chunk white tuna**	2
1 cup	**Shredded provolone or part-skim mozzarella cheese**	250 mL
1 cup	**Diced sweet red or green pepper**	250 mL
½ cup	**Light mayonnaise**	125 mL

1. Split rolls and arrange, cut side down, on rimmed
   baking sheet; broil until crisp and golden. Remove
   from oven; turn right side up and let cool.

2. Drain tuna and place in bowl. Add cheese, red
   pepper and mayonnaise; stir to mix well. Spread
   over rolls; sprinkle with pinch of pepper.

3. Broil about 6 inches (15 cm) from heat for about
   3 minutes or until cheese is melted and filling is
   golden and hot throughout.

Cheese Tips

Both mozzarella and provolone are stretchy cheeses ideal for sandwich melts and
pizzas. The advantage of the mozzarella is its availability. Mild, it has kid appeal
and gives buyers the option of using a lower-fat version. Provolone has an up side,
too — and that just happens to be taste, with calories and grams of fat actu-
ally counting for satisfaction.

MENU

Grilled Vegetable "Strollers"

Cantaloupe Wedges with Lime

TIP

Hummus is a thick sauce made from mashed chick-peas seasoned with lemon juice, garlic and oil. It is available in Middle Eastern food stores and some supermarkets.

•

You can grill other vegetables, such as diagonally sliced zucchini or sweet Spanish, Vidalia or Texas onions, brushed lightly with olive oil.

Grilled Vegetable "Strollers"

"Strollers" are great for a picnic or backyard supper when holding your food in your hand and eating from the top down is just fine.

1	Eggplant (1 lb/500 g)	1
2	Sweet red peppers	2
8	8-inch (20 cm) flour tortillas	8
1/2 cup	Prepared hummus	125 mL
1	Bunch arugula or watercress, coarse stems removed	1

1. Cut eggplant crosswise into 1/2-inch (1 cm) thick slices; sprinkle lightly with salt. Layer in colander; let stand for 30 minutes. Rinse and pat dry. Brush all over with 1 tbsp (15 mL) olive oil; sprinkle with 1/4 tsp (1 mL) pepper.

2. Place eggplant and red peppers on greased grill over high heat or under broiler; cook for 20 minutes or until eggplant is well marked and soft and peppers are blistered and darkened. Transfer to separate plates.

3. Peel red peppers; core and remove seeds. Cut each into 6 strips.

4. Meanwhile, wrap tortillas in foil; heat in 350°F (180°C) oven for 10 minutes or until warmed.

5. Lay tortillas on work surface; spread top two-thirds with hummus. Arrange 2 strips of red pepper and equal amount of eggplant and arugula in centre of tortilla on hummus. Sprinkle with pinch each salt and pepper, if desired. Fold up bottom, pressing firmly; fold over each side to make snug roll. Fasten with toothpicks, if desired.

MAKES 4 SERVINGS

PER SERVING	
calories	460
protein	14 g
fat	15 g
carbohydrate	71 g
source of fibre	very high
source of calcium	good
source of iron	excellent

MENU

Chicken Gyros

Tabbouleh or Couscous Salad

TIP

Pita breads are also excellent pockets for this filling. You can line the pockets with lettuce to help prevent leaks.

•

Tzatziki sauce is thick yogurt with lemon, garlic and cucumber. Look for this Greek specialty in the dairy case. Or substitute thick yogurt and add minced garlic and sliced cucumber to your gyros.

Chicken Gyros

Whether you pronounce these juicy sandwiches "yee-roh" or "jeer-oh," you will enjoy how fast, filling and delicious they are for weeknight suppers. Good in the winter, gyros are even better in the summer and make perfect patio food.

4	8-inch (20 cm) flour tortillas	4
2	Small tomatoes	2
1	Large onion	1
1 lb	Boneless skinless chicken breasts	500 g
½ cup	Prepared tzatziki sauce	125 mL

1. Wrap tortillas in foil; heat in 350°F (180°C) oven for 10 minutes or until warmed through.

2. Meanwhile, core tomatoes; chop coarsely. Cut onion into quarters; slice thinly crosswise. Set aside. Using chef's knife, cut chicken across the grain into thin strips.

3. In nonstick skillet, heat 1 tsp (5 mL) vegetable oil over medium-high heat. Add chicken; sprinkle with pinch each salt and pepper. Cook, stirring, for about 5 minutes or until chicken is no longer pink inside.

4. Spread tzatziki sauce evenly over tortillas. Mound chicken, tomatoes and onion evenly in centre of each. Fold up bottom of tortilla, then sides, to enclose filling.

MAKES 4 SERVINGS

PER SERVING	
calories	380
protein	35 g
fat	8 g
carbohydrate	41 g
source of calcium	good
source of iron	good

Eggs

Eggs

Egg TIPS

- *An egg is an excellent food value. It has about 80 calories and six grams of fat, both of which are found mostly in the yolk, along with cholesterol (about 272 milligrams).*

- *Eggs are classified by weight. At Canadian Living, recipes are created using large eggs. When serving children, a medium or small egg is a good idea.*

- *There is no nutritional or taste difference between white and brown eggs. The color of the shell is due to the breed of chicken.*

- *Buy eggs at a refrigerated source and store them in the refrigerator, never at room temperature. Always check the best-before date on the carton.*

- *Store eggs, large end up, in their egg carton in the coldest part of the refrigerator. Taking eggs out of the carton exposes them to refrigerator odors, which their porous shells absorb. Storing them in the refrigerator door's egg keeper shortens their shelf life, because the inside of the door is the warmest part of the refrigerator. The jiggling as the door opens and closes exposes the eggs to possible breakage.*

▼ HOME FRIES FRITTATA
(RECIPE, PAGE 85)

- *To save leftover egg yolks, cover them with water in an airtight container to use within three days. To freeze for up to six months, add a pinch of salt or 1-1/2 tsp (7 mL) granulated sugar or corn syrup per 1/4 cup (50 mL) yolks.*

- *To save leftover egg whites, cover them tightly and use within four days or freeze for up to six months. Thaw in refrigerator.*

MENU

Saucy Pasta Frittata

Whole Wheat Pita Breads

Spinach and Mushroom Salad

TIP

If your skillet does not have an ovenproof handle, wrap it in foil to prevent scorching.

For a "pizza," sprinkle the frittata with some mozzarella cheese just before broiling.

To make pasta especially for this frittata, cook about 1-¼ cups (300 mL) fusilli.

Saucy Pasta Frittata

Here's a great way to use up leftover pasta and sauce.

1	Onion, chopped	1
1	Zucchini, chopped	1
2 cups	Cooked short pasta (fusilli or shells)	500 mL
2 cups	Meatless spaghetti sauce	500 mL
8	Eggs	8

1. In 10-inch (25 cm) nonstick skillet with ovenproof handle, heat 1 tbsp (15 mL) olive oil over medium heat; cook onion and zucchini for 5 minutes, stirring often.

2. Add pasta; cook, stirring occasionally, for 5 minutes or just until vegetables are tender and pasta is lightly browned.

3. Stir in 1 cup (250 mL) of the sauce; reduce heat to medium-low.

4. Whisk eggs lightly; season with ¼ tsp (1 mL) each salt and pepper. Pour over pasta mixture, lifting some of the mixture to let eggs flow underneath. Cover and cook over medium heat for about 5 minutes or until bottom is set.

5. Pour remaining sauce over top. Broil for about 4 minutes or until top is crisped and eggs are set. Let stand for 2 minutes before cutting into wedges.

MAKES 6 SERVINGS

PER SERVING	
calories	275
protein	12 g
fat	12 g
carbohydrate	30 g

step by step

In nonstick skillet with ovenproof handle, cook onions and thyme in a little olive oil until softened.

Add potatoes; cook, stirring occasionally, until most of the cubes have crusty golden brown edges.

Add peas, stirring to distribute evenly.

Pour lightly beaten eggs over potato mixture, lifting edges to let egg flow underneath.

Broil until top is crisped and eggs are set. Let stand for 3 minutes. Invert onto platter.

Cut frittata into wedges to serve.

Home Fries Frittata

Here's a dish that's great for breakfast, brunch, lunch and dinner. In order to make it more often, it's worthwhile cooking a few extra potatoes one day for this frittata the next.

1	Onion, chopped	1
³/₄ tsp	Dried thyme	4 mL
3 cups	Cooked cubed potatoes (3 large)	750 mL
1 cup	Frozen peas	250 mL
6	Eggs	6

1. In 10-inch (25 cm) nonstick skillet with ovenproof handle, heat 2 tbsp (25 mL) olive oil over medium heat; cook onion and thyme, stirring often, for about 4 minutes or until softened.

2. Stir in potatoes; cook, turning a few times, for about 5 minutes or until most have crusty golden brown edges or sides. Stir in peas.

3. In bowl, beat eggs lightly; season with ¼ tsp (1 mL) each salt and pepper. Pour over potato mixture, lifting some of the mixture to let eggs flow underneath. Cook for about 5 minutes or until bottom is set.

4. Broil for about 4 minutes or until top is crisped and eggs are set. Let stand for 3 minutes. Invert onto platter; cut into wedges.

MAKES 6 SERVINGS

PER SERVING	
calories	210
protein	9 g
fat	10 g
carbohydrate	21 g

MENU

Crustless Mushroom Quiche

Green Salad with Tomatoes

TIP

Always store mushrooms, unwashed, in a paper bag in the refrigerator and use them as soon as possible.

•

To prevent mushrooms from absorbing water, just wipe individually with a damp cloth instead of rinsing them in water.

•

Portobello, crimini, portobellini and shiitake mushrooms are all good varieties to try. If using shiitake mushrooms, trim off stems because they are tough.

MAKES 4 SERVINGS

PER SERVING	
calories	255
protein	19 g
fat	17 g
carbohydrate	5 g
source of calcium	good

Crustless Mushroom Quiche

One healthful way to enjoy the convenience and pleasing taste of quiche is to forgo the crust. You won't miss it with meaty mushrooms studding the light cheese and egg custard.

2 cups	Sliced mushrooms (5 oz/150 g)	500 mL
8	Eggs	8
¾ cup	Milk	175 mL
2 tsp	Dijon mustard	10 mL
½ cup	Shredded light Swiss cheese	125 mL

1. In skillet, heat 1 tbsp (15 mL) extra-virgin olive oil over medium-high heat; cook mushrooms, stirring occasionally, until edges are browned and liquid is evaporated. Transfer to lightly greased 9-inch (23 cm) pie plate.

2. In bowl, whisk together eggs, milk, mustard and ¼ tsp (1 mL) each salt and pepper. Pour over mushrooms. Sprinkle with cheese.

3. Bake in 325°F (160°C) oven for 35 to 40 minutes or until tip of pointed knife inserted in centre comes out clean. Let stand for 3 minutes before serving.

Cheese Strata

*Fresh Tomato Salsa or
Tomato Salad*

TIP

Choose homemade-style bread because it doesn't turn to mush when soaked. When using smoked salmon, choose rye bread. For extra flavor with the red peppers, choose onion or cheese buns, focaccia, or pesto or olive loaf.

Cheese Strata

Strata is basically just eggs, milk, cheese and bread. But when you add ingredients such as roasted peppers, diced smoked ham or slivered smoked salmon, and cooked asparagus, peas or broccoli and bake it until puffed and crusty golden, a strata is as variable as you like. Here's the basic one to build on.

8 cups	Small cubes bread	2 L
1-1/2 cups	Shredded light Jarlsberg or Swiss cheese	375 mL
2	Sweet red peppers, roasted and diced (see Roasted Peppers, page 31)	2
4	Eggs	4
2 cups	Milk	500 mL

1. Lightly grease 11- by 7-inch (2 L) glass baking dish. Sprinkle in half of the bread, then half of the cheese. Sprinkle with all but 1/4 cup (50 mL) of the red peppers. Cover with remaining bread and shredded cheese.

2. In bowl, whisk together eggs, milk and 1/4 tsp (1 mL) each salt and pepper. Pour over strata; press lightly so that bread absorbs egg mixture. Cover and refrigerate for at least 1 hour or for up to 24 hours.

3. Sprinkle with reserved red peppers. Bake in 350°F (180°C) oven for about 50 minutes or until puffed, crusty and golden. Serve immediately.

MAKES 8 SERVINGS

PER SERVING

calories	220
protein	15 g
fat	8 g
carbohydrate	21 g
source of calcium	excellent

MENU

Corn Soufflé Squares

Cabbage and Apple Slaw

TIP

To reduce fat, look for light versions of cheese.

•

When beating egg whites, start with eggs at room temperature (warm under warm water if necessary) and use a clean bowl and beaters.

•

Creamed corn does not contain cream or any other dairy product. The word "creamed" refers to its texture — made by puréeing some of the kernels.

Corn Soufflé Squares

In a five-ingredient soufflé, creamed corn does double duty — it's the star flavor and provides the liquid. Serve this mild-flavored soufflé with a piquant salad and pass chili sauce or salsa.

2 tbsp	Butter	25 mL
2 tbsp	All-purpose flour	25 mL
1	Can (14 oz/398 mL) creamed corn	1
5	Eggs, separated	5
2/3 cup	Shredded light old Cheddar-style cheese	150 mL

1. In heavy saucepan, melt butter over medium heat; stir in flour and 1/4 tsp (1 mL) pepper for 1 minute without browning.

2. Whisk in corn and 1/4 cup (50 mL) water, stirring until thickened and boiling. Remove from heat.

3. Whisk in egg yolks, 1 at a time. Stir in half of the cheese.

4. In separate bowl, beat egg whites until stiff peaks form. Stir about one-quarter into corn mixture. Scrape corn mixture over remaining whites and fold together.

5. Scrape into greased 11- by 7-inch (2 L) baking dish. Sprinkle with remaining cheese. Bake in 400°F (200°C) oven for 20 to 25 minutes or until puffed and golden. Serve immediately.

MAKES 6 SERVINGS

PER SERVING

calories	195
protein	10 g
fat	11 g
carbohydrate	16 g

Stews

Stews

▼ BEEF STEW WITH GNOCCHI DUMPLINGS
(RECIPE, PAGE 93)

Stew TIPS

• *There are many ways to thicken a stew. Cook a potato or sweet potato along with other ingredients and mash it into the juices. Shake flour with cold water and stir it into the stew near the end of cooking time. Make a* beurre manié *by blending equal amounts of butter or oil with flour, then whisking by small spoonfuls into simmering stew until thickened to taste.*

• *Make stews ahead of time and chill overnight. Then it's easy to lift off solidified fat, and the time mellows and blends the flavors.*

• *Add variety to stews with frozen mixed vegetables, or include a few leftover vegetables if they suit the stew's flavor.*

• *Freshen the flavors of stew by stirring in a little dried or fresh herbs at the end of cooking time.*

• *A splash of vinegar or lemon juice complements the sweet flavors of carrots and onions in a stew. Taste the stew before serving to determine if this tart touch is in order.*

• *Vary the liquid in a stew; stock (unsalted if possible), beer, wine, and juices such as apple and tomato are well suited to stews.*

• *Trim off fat from meat before browning.*

• *Serve stews in edible containers such as roasted acorn squash halves or a soup bowl lined with mashed potatoes, rice or popovers.*

• *Reheat individual portions of stew in the microwave. You can also freeze stews (without potatoes) in bowls to thaw and reheat for quick cold-weather comfort food.*

MENU

Smoky Baked Beans and Sausage

Crusty Whole Wheat Kaisers

Tossed Green Salad

TIP

Look for Russian-style sweet prepared mustard. A popular quality brand is Canadian-made Honeycup. Avoid mustards called honey mustard if they are a bright yellow color because they often have a harsh flavor that overpowers the bite of the mustard and the soothing quality of its sweetness.

MAKES 6 SERVINGS

PER SERVING

calories	620
protein	28 g
fat	22 g
carbohydrate	77 g
source of fibre	very high
source of calcium	good
source of iron	excellent

Smoky Baked Beans and Sausage

This rich and smoky dish is a memorable way to welcome everyone home after a bitterly cold day at work or school, or after a vigorous workout on the slopes — or, in the real world, with a snow shovel.

2-$\frac{1}{2}$ cups	Navy (white pea) beans (1 lb/500 g)	625 mL
1-$\frac{1}{2}$ cups	Salsa or chili sauce	375 mL
$\frac{1}{2}$ cup	Fancy molasses	125 mL
2 tbsp	Sweet mustard	25 mL
1 lb	Smoked sausages (such as chorizo)	500 g

1. In Dutch oven or large saucepan, cover beans with 3 times their volume of water; let stand overnight. (Or bring to boil and boil for 2 minutes; cover and let stand for 1 hour.) Drain beans.

2. In same pot, combine beans with 8 cups (2 L) cold water; bring to boil. Reduce heat, cover and simmer for 30 to 45 minutes or until tender; drain.

3. In same pot, combine beans, salsa, molasses, mustard and 3-$\frac{1}{2}$ cups (875 mL) water. Nestle sausages into mixture. Cover and bake in 300°F (150°C) oven for 2-$\frac{1}{2}$ hours.

4. Uncover and bake for 1 to 1-$\frac{1}{2}$ hours longer or until beans are very tender, adding up to $\frac{1}{2}$ cup (125 mL) water if sauce becomes too thick.

5. Remove sausages; cut into bite-size pieces and return to pan. Season with pinch of pepper.

step by step

Brown beef, in batches, in oil over medium-high heat. Transfer browned pieces to plate.

Add onions and two-thirds of the oregano; cook until lightly browned and softened.

Return beef to pan, along with any accumulated juices.

Add water, salt and pepper. Bring to boil. Reduce heat, cover and simmer until beef is tender.

Add gnocchi and bring to boil; cook, uncovered, until sauce is thickened.

Add frozen vegetables; simmer, stirring frequently, until piping hot.

Beef Stew with Gnocchi Dumplings

If you like dumplings, you will enjoy how effortless it is to have gnocchi-style dumplings in this robust stew.

2 lb	Lean stew beef, cut in 1-inch (2.5 cm) cubes	1 kg
4	Onions, quartered	4
1 tbsp	Dried oregano, basil or Italian herb seasoning	15 mL
1	Pkg (1 lb/454 g) frozen or fresh gnocchi	1
1	Pkg (300 g) frozen mixed chopped vegetables	1

1. In large Dutch oven, heat 2 tbsp (25 mL) vegetable oil over medium-high heat; brown beef, in 4 batches and adding a bit more oil if needed. Transfer browned pieces to plate.

2. Drain off any fat in pan. Add onions and 2 tsp (10 mL) of the oregano; cook, stirring occasionally, for about 6 minutes or until lightly browned and softened.

3. Return beef to pan. Add 3 cups (750 mL) water, $3/4$ tsp (4 mL) salt and $1/2$ tsp (2 mL) pepper; bring to boil. Reduce heat to low; cover and simmer for about 1-$1/2$ hours or until beef is tender.

4. Stir in gnocchi and bring to boil; boil gently, uncovered, for 8 minutes or until sauce is thickened.

5. Stir in frozen vegetables and remaining oregano. Simmer, stirring often, until piping hot.

MAKES 6 SERVINGS

PER SERVING	
calories	510
protein	40 g
fat	16 g
carbohydrate	52 g
source of fibre	very high
source of iron	excellent

Vaguely Coq au Vin

Special enough for your favorite people and impressive even after 30 years of enthusiastic French cooking in Canadian kitchens, this browned then wine-simmered chicken is a dish every cook should have in his or her repertoire.

8	Chicken thighs (2 lb/1 kg total)	8
¼ cup	All-purpose flour	50 mL
2-¼ tsp	Dried thyme	11 mL
6	Small onions, quartered	6
1 cup	Dry white wine	250 mL

1. Pull skin off chicken thighs. In bag, shake together flour, 2 tsp (10 mL) of the thyme and ½ tsp (2 mL) each salt and pepper. Add chicken, in batches, and shake to coat.

2. In large nonstick skillet or Dutch oven, heat 1 tbsp (15 mL) olive oil over medium-high heat; brown chicken well on both sides. Transfer to plate.

3. Drain off fat in skillet; reduce heat to medium. Add onions; cook, stirring occasionally, for 5 minutes or until golden and softened.

4. Return chicken to skillet; pour wine over top. Cover and simmer, turning once, for about 20 minutes or until juices run clear when chicken is pierced. Transfer to warm platter and keep warm.

5. Add remaining thyme and ¼ tsp (1 mL) each salt and pepper to pan juices; boil for about 5 minutes or until thickened. Pour over chicken.

Quick Curried Shrimp

Curry is a combination of spices that is garnering more and more enthusiasts in Canada. Here, curry paste makes a full-flavored dish that's easy and impressive.

1 tbsp	Indian curry paste	15 mL
1	Onion, chopped	1
3/4 cup	Coconut milk	175 mL
2 cups	Small cauliflower florets or snow peas	500 mL
1 lb	Large shrimp, peeled and deveined	500 mL

1. In heavy saucepan, heat 1 tbsp (15 mL) vegetable oil over medium heat; stir in curry paste for about 30 seconds or until broken up and darkened slightly.

2. Add onion; cook, stirring often, for about 5 minutes or until softened. Pour in coconut milk; cook for 3 minutes or until slightly thickened.

3. Add cauliflower; bring to boil. Reduce heat, cover and simmer for about 7 minutes or until cauliflower is tender-crisp.

4. Add shrimp and increase heat to medium-high; cook, stirring, for 3 to 4 minutes or until shrimp are bright pink and firm and cauliflower is tender.

MAKES 4 SERVINGS

PER SERVING	
calories	275
protein	25 g
fat	16 g
carbohydrate	8 g
source of iron	excellent

INDEX